Edexcel GCSE

History A: The Making of the Modern World

Unit 3B War and the transformation of British society c.1931–51

Student Book

Jane Shuter
Series editors: Nigel Kelly • Angela Leonard

A PEARSON COMPANY

Contents: delivering the Edexcel GCSE History A (The Making of the Modern World) specification Unit 3B

Welcome to the course

Welcome to Modern World History! Studying this subject will help you to understand the world you live in: the events of the last hundred years can help to explain the problems and opportunities that exist in the world today.

How to use this book

There are four units in the course and each is worth 25% of the whole GCSE. This book covers Unit 3B: War and the transformation of British society c.1931–51. There are four key topics in this unit and you will study *all four*.

- **Key Topic 1:** The impact of the Depression
- **Key Topic 2:** Britain alone
- **Key Topic 3:** Britain at war
- **Key Topic 4:** Labour in power 1945–51

exam **zone**

Zone in: how to get into the perfect 'zone' for revision.

Planning zone: tips and advice on how to plan revision effectively.

Know zone: the facts you need to know, memory tips and exam-style practice for every section.

Don't panic zone: last-minute revision tips.

Exam zone: what to expect on the exam paper.

Zone out: what happens after the exams.

ResultsPlus

Top Tips provide examiner advice and guidance to help improve your results.

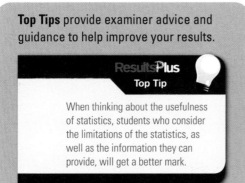

ResultsPlus
Top Tip

When thinking about the usefulness of statistics, students who consider the limitations of the statistics, as well as the information they can provide, will get a better mark.

ResultsPlus
Watch out!

Don't be confused by the use of the word 'idleness' in the report and elsewhere. It did not mean laziness – although it was sometimes also used in that way, especially by people who wanted to criticise the unemployed. It meant being out of work.

Watch out! These warn you about common mistakes and misconceptions that examiners frequently see students make.

Build better answers give an opportunity to answer exam-style questions. They include tips for what a basic or incorrect ■, good ● and excellent △ answer will contain.

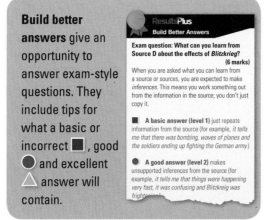

ResultsPlus
Build Better Answers

Exam question: What can you learn from Source D about the effects of *Blitzkrieg*?
(6 marks)

When you are asked what you can learn from a source or sources, you are expected to make *inferences*. This means you work something out from the information in the source; you don't just copy it.

■ **A basic answer (level 1)** just repeats information from the source (for example, *it tells me that there was bombing, waves of planes and the soldiers ending up fighting the German army.*)

● **A good answer (level 2)** makes unsupported inferences from the source (for example, *it tells me that things were happening very fast, it was confusing and Blitzkreig was frightening.*)

Maximise your marks are featured in the Know Zone at the end of each section. They include an exam-style question with a student answer, examiner comments and an improved answer so that you can see how to build a better response.

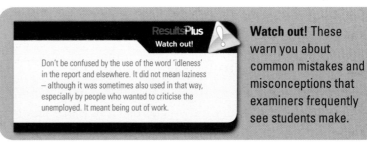

ResultsPlus
Maximise your marks

Question 3
Examiner's tip: Question 3 will ask you to use three sources and consider the extent to which they say the same thing or support a statement. So the question tests cross-referencing sources.
In the exam, there are two slightly different question types used to test this skill. You might be asked 'Do these sources support the view that…?' or you could be asked 'How far do these sources agree about…? (10 marks). Whichever question is asked, the same mark scheme will be used. Let's look at an example (Sources A, B and C on pages 38–39). 'Do Sources A, B, and C support the view that the local response to the bombing of Coventry was well organised?' (10 marks)

Student answer	Examiner comment
The sources show that the bombing was awful but the local authorities got on with dealing with it. OR I don't think that they show that. There were huge amounts of mess.	These are two different level 1 answers. Level 1 answers decide that the sources either support or do not support the view under discussion and don't use information from the sources to back up what they say.

Unit 3: The source enquiry: an introduction

What is Unit 3 about?

The Unit 3 topics are very different from those in Units 1 and 2. To start with, you are never going to be asked to just recall historical information you have learned. If you find yourself sitting in an examination telling the story of what happened in a particular historical event, you are almost certainly not doing the right thing! Unlike Units 1 and 2, Unit 3 is not about recalling or describing key features. Nor is it about using your knowledge to construct an argument about why things happened – or what the consequences of an action were. Instead, Unit 3 topics are about understanding the importance of sources in the study of history.

History as a subject is not just about learning a series of facts and repeating them in an examination. It is actually a process of enquiry. Historians understand that our historical knowledge comes from evidence from the past ('sources'). Historians have to piece together what has happened in the past from these sources. They need to interpret the sources to build up the historical picture. That is what you will be looking at in Unit 3.

Since sources can sometimes be interpreted in a number of ways, historians also have to make judgments about the usefulness of information in sources (utility) and whether these sources are giving us an accurate picture (reliability).

Of course, you cannot interpret sources or make judgments about their utility or reliability unless you know about the topic they relate to. That is why you do have to use your knowledge in an examination. You don't use it to tell the story, but you do use it to make judgments about sources. So for your Unit 3 topic, make sure you learn your information, but even more importantly, make sure you use it to make judgments about the sources. There are very few marks in this unit for factual recall!

The examination

In the examination you will be given a collection of six to eight sources to study. Then you will be asked five questions. These five questions will test your understanding of interpreting sources. The good news is that each year the individual questions will always test the same skill. So question 1 will always be about making an inference. The table at the top of the next page shows how this works.

Question	Marks	Type of question
1	6	Making inferences from sources
2	8	Considering the purpose of a source
3	10	Cross-referencing sources
4	10	Evaluating the utility or reliability of sources
5	16	Evaluating a hypothesis

So before you study the historical topic from which your sources will be drawn, let's make sure you know how to answer each question type.

Making inferences from sources

When you read or look at a source and you understand its content, you are 'comprehending' that source. When you make a judgment from what the source says or shows, that is 'making an inference'. Let us look at a source to see what that means.

Source A From a book about the *Jarrow Crusade*, written by a historian in 2005.

> The Jarrow Crusade was one of four hunger marches to London in 1936. They were: the National Hunger March, the Jarrow Crusade, the National League of the Blind march and the Scottish veterans' march. They passed through the same towns and sometimes crossed paths. They were ignored in the same way by the government and were all carefully watched by the police.

In the examination, the sort of question you might be asked would be:

'*What can you learn from this source about unemployment in 1936?*'

You could say: '*People went on hunger marches.*' That is true, but it doesn't take much working out, does it? It isn't an inference either, because that is exactly what the source says.

An example of an inference about unemployment would be: '*Unemployment must have been a serious problem because the source says there were four different hunger marches. That suggests people had no money for food because they were not working – and the number of marches suggests a lot of unemployment.*' Can you see the difference?

Considering the purpose of a source

It is important for historians to understand why sources have been created. Sometimes people are just recording what has happened (as in a diary), but sometimes they are created to get a message across. For example, when an artist paints a picture, he or she may be doing so in order to get a message across. Let's look at an example.

| Source B | A painting of the Jarrow Crusade, painted by art student Colin Moss in 1936. Moss came from a working-class background and believed in social reform. |

In the examination, the sort of question you might be asked about this painting is:

'Why do you think the artist painted this picture?'

You could say: 'to show the Jarrow March', but that is a very weak answer. A good answer would be to look at the detail in the poster and work out why paint this march and why paint a hunger march at all? You need to consider the artist's purpose. You could start with the message he's sending. The men are marching away from the picture. You don't see their faces, but they are marching and look determined and organised. The policeman isn't having to do anything to control them.

So by the way the artist shows them (including the rain; it didn't rain every day) the artist wants you to feel sympathy for the marchers, to feel supportive. The caption tells you he's a working-class student who supported social reform, so this confirms the purpose is that he wants sympathy for the marchers.

Cross-referencing sources

Question 3 asks you to interpret the information and tone of three sources and consider the degree to which they are saying the same thing. So the question tests cross-reference. Let's use Source B and add another two.

| Source C | Part of a speech given to the Jarrow marchers by the Reverend Thomas at Northallerton. The town council had not sent anyone to greet them. |

I don't think the decision of the council not to welcome the marchers represents the feeling of the people of Northallerton. This march is the finest organised I have ever seen. It is our duty to spare no effort to help our unfortunate comrades and I think the churches of this country should have led the march and taken it right to London as an appeal not only to the Government but also to the common humanity in man.

| Source D | A government statement made during the marches. |

Ministers have considered the fact that there are a number of 'marches' on London in progress or being planned. In the opinion of the government these marches can do no good for the causes they say they represent and are likely to cause unnecessary hardship for those taking part in them. Processions to London cannot have any right in our democracy to influence government policy.

In the examination, the sort of question you might be asked is:

'How far do these sources agree about the Jarrow Crusade? Explain your answer.'

Your task is to study them and say how they do or do not agree. In this case, you are going to be looking at support for the marchers or the lack of it. There might well be evidence of both in one source, so read them carefully.

Evaluating the utility or reliability of sources

You have to make sure you understand the difference between utility (usefulness) and reliability (accuracy). Remember:

● usefulness is about what you can find out from a source
● reliability is whether you can believe it.

Let's look again at Source C to demonstrate this.

In the examination, the sort of question you might be asked is:

'How useful is this source for a historian studying the hunger marches?' (In the exam you will be looking at two sources, not just one.)

You could say: *'It is very useful because it shows how people felt about the hunger marches. It is especially useful because it shows that there were supporters and people against them, even in the same town.'* But you would need to address reliability here too, even though the source seems to show there is both support and a lack of it. The speaker, a vicar, gives the impression that the council was wrong not to welcome the marchers, that this lack of welcome was confined to only a few people. This suggests he was biased in favour of the marchers.

Evaluating a hypothesis

In the examination, the final question will ask you to consider whether the six sources given support a hypothesis. Here we will use five, but you can still see how to do the question from these.

Source E *A poster from the election in 1951.*

In the examination, the sort of question you might be asked is:

"There were several hunger marches in the 1930s; the Jarrow one was nothing special." How far do the sources in this paper support this statement? Use details from the sources and your own knowledge to explain your answer.'

So now you need to consider the sources individually and see which side of the argument you would put them on. Don't forget that you should also think about the reliability of the sources. What is your decision?

Key Topic 1: The impact of the Depression

In 1929, the US stock market collapsed. The USA had been supporting the European economy since the First World War ended in 1918. Now, the USA had to trade less, stop lending and call for the repayment of its loans to other countries. Britain was among these countries. The Depression in the USA had a terrible effect on some parts of Britain's economy. Industries sold less, therefore made less money, so had to sack workers or pay them considerably less and restrict their working hours. This produced a downward economic spiral where these problems fed each other over and over again. One of the most obvious signs of this was the rise in unemployment.

In this Key Topic, you will study:

- the growth of unemployment and the government response
- the experience of the unemployed
- case study: the Jarrow Crusade.

You will see how unemployment was different in different industries and parts of Britain. You will also see how the unemployed campaigned for work (stressing that it was work they wanted, not more benefits). You will consider the action the government took to help the unemployed – and the effects of their actions.

Your case study of the Jarrow Crusade will examine the Crusade itself as well as opposition and public reaction to it. It will also consider why the Crusade was so important.

Britain in the 1920s: background to the Depression

At the end of the First World War, the only financial help for the unemployed was National Insurance Benefit, set up in 1911 to cover workers in a few industries, such as shipbuilding, where work was not steady. Workers and their employers paid into an Unemployment Fund. If work dried up, the fund paid benefit for up to 15 weeks. In November 1918, the government set up an Out-of-Work Donation Scheme (often called 'the dole'), which paid a small amount of benefit. The scheme was set up to help returning soldiers and war workers who could not find employment. During the 1920s, the economy was struggling and unemployment was a problem. Although women had worked during the war, they were expected to give up their jobs to the returning men. Most workers, and therefore most of the unemployed, were men – often men with families to support.

The **Depression** made unemployment in Britain worse. In 1929, there were 1.5 million unemployed. In 1930, it had risen to 2.4 million. Some newer industries, such as car and electrical goods manufacturing, did hire more workers – but were mainly based in the south and west of the country. Workers in badly affected industries and the unemployed protested in various ways. They collected petitions and wrote individually to the government, asking for work. They wrote to the newspapers, highlighting the problems. They also regularly marched to London to protest to the government about conditions. These '**hunger marches**' were almost all organised by the National Unemployed Workers' Movement, (NUWM) which was set up in 1921. They tried hard to make the point that the unemployed were not lazy, but wanted work more than **benefits**. Meanwhile, the state, and the Unemployment Fund, were paying out more and more money in various benefits, as work was not to be found.

> **Source A**
> *Welsh miners photographed in November 1927, on their arrival in London to protest about the government (led by Stanley Baldwin) extending miners' legal working hours from 7 hours to 8 hours a day. Think about why the man to the right of the banner is wearing his medals.*

Examination question

What was the purpose of Source A? Use details of the photograph and your own knowledge to answer this question. (8 marks)

> **Source B**
> *A song sung by striking clothing workers, mostly women, in London in 1928. To 'stick' was to stay out on strike, not return to work.*

We've never had decent wages
And always done our work well
How long must this go on?
More work – less pay
But every dog will have its day
We'll stick, by gum, by golly
The bosses they'll be sorry.

Unemployment in Britain in the 1930s

> ## Learning objectives
>
> In this chapter you will learn about:
> - levels and distribution of unemployment in Britain in the 1930s
> - making inferences from sources.

Unemployment in the 1930s was highest in the coal, iron and steel, cotton and shipbuilding industries, in the north and east of England and in Scotland and Wales. By 1932, 34.5% of miners were unemployed and 62% of all shipbuilders. Unemployment was not spread evenly. When pits and shipyards closed, the villages that served them became almost entirely unemployed.

Meanwhile, 80% of all new factories built from 1932 to 1937 were in London or nearby. They were usually new industries, such as car making. These factories ran mostly on electricity, not coal, so did not help the coal industry by increasing demand for fuel. But they did keep employment up in London and the south east. The chemical industry, for example, had 17.6% unemployment in 1932, which was low compared to mining or shipbuilding. If you lived in the right part of the country and worked in the right industry, the Depression could almost pass you by.

ResultsPlus
Top Tip

When thinking about the usefulness of statistics, students who consider the limitations of the statistics, as well as the information they can provide, will get a better mark.

| Source A | Unemployment in Britain, 1920–38. |

Date	Unemployed, on National Insurance	Total unemployed	Total unemployed as % of all those able to work
1929	1,250,000	1,503,000	8%
1930	1,979,000	2,379,000	12.3%
1931	2,705,000	3,252,000	16.4%
1932	2,828,000	3,400,000	17%
1933	2,567,000	3,087,000	15.4%
1934	2,170,000	2,609,000	12.9%
1935	2,027,000	2,437,000	12%
1936	1,749,000	2,100,000	10.2%
1937	1,482,000	1,776,000	8.5%
1938	1,800,000	2,164,000	10.1%

Source: W. R. Garside British Unemployment 1919-1939, (1990), Table 2, p.5 (adapted), © Cambridge University Press 1990, reproduced with permission.

| Source B | From a 1973 interview with Richard Etheridge, who became a union leader in the Austin car factory in Birmingham in the 1940s. |

I grew up in Birmingham during the Depression. Out of a class of 30 of us boys, we were lucky if one got a job when they left. I worked for a while in a laboratory, making up formulas for various industries. I got very sick of that. Then our family started up an all-night café and I left to work there. I started to meet people involved in the **trade union** movement and got interested in that.

| Source C | From a 1996 interview with Con Dawson, who was in her twenties in the 1930s. What do you think she meant by the last sentence? |

I worked as a secretary for the record company HMV in their London office. The Depression never touched us, though I do remember hanging out of my office window to watch one of the hunger marches. We all felt sorry for the poor men, but it wasn't anything to do with us, really.

| Source D | The percentage of people paying National Insurance in each region who were able to work but were unemployed, 1929–38. |

Date	London	South east	South west	Midlands	North east	North west	Scotland	Wales
1929	5.6	5.6	8.1	9.3	13.7	13.3	12.1	19.3
1930	8.1	8	10.4	14.7	20.2	23.8	18.5	25.9
1931	12.2	12	14.5	20.3	27.4	28.2	26.6	32.4
1932	13.5	14.3	17.1	20.1	28.5	25.8	27.7	36.5
1933	11.8	11.5	15.7	17.4	26	23.5	26.1	34.6
1934	9.2	8.7	13.1	12.9	22.1	20.8	23.1	32.3
1935	8.5	8.1	11.6	11.2	20.7	19.7	21.3	31.2
1936	7.2	7.3	9.4	9.2	16.8	17.1	18.7	29.4
1937	6.4	6.7	7.8	7.3	11.1	14	16	23.3
1938	8	8	8.2	10.3	13.6	17.9	16.4	24.8

| Source E | A hunger march in London in 1930. This march was organised by the National Unemployed Workers' Movement (NUWM). What do you think the slogan means? |

Activities

1   a   What can you learn from Source A about unemployment in Britain in the 1930s?

    b   Write a sentence explaining how Source C extends your knowledge about unemployment in the 1930s.

    c   Use Source D to make a graph of unemployment in Britain in the 1930s.

    d   Write a sentence explaining the patterns the graph shows.

2   Write a piece of advice to someone time-travelling back to live in the 1930s for a few years. Tell them which part of the country to live in and why.

Government reactions

12

> **Learning objectives**
>
> In this chapter you will learn about:
> - how the government tried to deal with the problems of unemployment
> - cross-referencing sources
> - considering the purpose of a source.

Labour in power

In 1929, Labour came to power, with Ramsey MacDonald as prime minister. The government needed money. It was in debt and the Depression made it hard to borrow money to cover its spending. It made huge spending cuts, for example cutting the wages of government workers by 10–15%. It did not have the money to cover 1929 unemployment rates – and it was clear those rates would rise. So, in August 1931, government **ministers** discussed a proposal to cut benefit rates by 15% and set up a means test. This test allowed officials to visit the benefit claimer's home, to examine his living conditions (to make sure he was poor enough) and to demand to know all savings and money earned by other family members. Most ministers refused to accept these proposals, saying they would cause too much hardship. The government collapsed.

The National Government

MacDonald, as prime minister, set up a National Government of moderate Labour, Liberal and Conservative MPs. The National Government held a general election in October – and won. It cut the benefit rate by 10%. Over the next few years, it passed laws to help the unemployed (see Source B). But rising unemployment meant that, while each person got less benefit, the government was still paying out more. Money for aid under the *Special Areas Act* was too little and too poorly distributed. Some places improved dramatically; others not at all. Also, some local employment offices were much more generous in the interpretation of the law than others, and gave benefits more freely.

Source A — *Part of a speech by Labour MP, George Lansbury, in a debate in parliament, 4 November 1932. Do you think Lansbury was in the National Government?*

The cost of unemployment, the £600 million or so, is a fraction of the real cost of unemployment to this nation. There is the cost to families and to individuals; all their savings poured out and gone. You cannot starve people (although it is semi-starvation for many now). I appeal to the Government. We think the amounts are too low, and should be increased. It is said we cannot afford it. We cannot afford the physical, mental and moral deterioration to people who cannot live on what is provided.

Source B — *Main changes and laws affecting the unemployed in the 1930s.*

1930 *Unemployment Insurance Act*: more people entitled to benefit; benefit claimers no longer have to prove they had been 'actively seeking work' (used to refuse many people benefit).

1931 *Means test*: introduced a benefit rate cut. In the first 10 weeks, 271,000 people failed the means test and could not longer claim benefit.

1934 *Unemployment Act*: made clear the division between National Insurance payments (a right) and the dole (based on need, which could be refused). National Unemployment Assistance Board was to run the dole from taxes.

1934 *Special Areas Act*: £2 million aid for Scotland, Tyneside (in the north east), Cumberland (in the north west) and South Wales.

1937 *Special Areas (Amendment) Act*: gave tax cuts and low rent and rates to businesses that moved into these areas.

Source C *A poster for the National Government for the 1935 election.*

Smokeless Chimneys and—
ANXIOUS MOTHERS!

THE REMEDY

VOTE FOR THE NATIONAL GOVERNMENT

Results Plus
Build Better Answers

Exam question: What was the purpose of Source C? Use details from the poster and your own knowledge to explain your answer. (8 marks)
The following will help you when answering an examination question similar to the one above about the *purpose* of a source.

■ **A basic answer (level 1)** makes a general statement, but does not refer to the sources or any other knowledge of the context (for example, *It wants people to vote for the National Government*).

● **A good answer (level 2)** considers the **message** of the source, using details from the source or context (for example, *The National Government will help mothers who can't afford to heat their homes: 'smokeless chimneys, anxious mothers'*).

▲ **An excellent answer (level 3)** explains the **purpose** of the source. (For example, *It seems to be targeted at women from poor families, or people sympathetic to them, to get them to vote for the National Government. It shows their plight and implies that the National Government will fix things.*)

Activities

1 Source C suggests the National Government is the answer to unemployment and the problems it brings. Write a sentence or two saying whether Source B supports this idea or not, giving examples from the source.

2 In groups, hold a five-minute mini-debate on the statement: 'The sources show that the National Government was just trying to save money, not help the unemployed.'

Results Plus
Watch out!

The benefit payment system was complicated. Don't confuse the benefit that a person got from their National Insurance (NI) contributions with the much lower 'dole' payment paid by the government. NI contributions were only paid for 15 weeks. The dole was for those not covered by NI, or still unemployed after 15 weeks. Dole claimers had to pass the 'humiliating' means test.

What was it like to be unemployed?

Learning objectives

In this chapter you will learn about:

● experiences of the unemployed
● evaluating the utility or reliability of sources.

In some ways, the experience of unemployment was the same for everyone. You never had enough money, so you were always making choices about spending – food or fuel or rent? You had to go to the **Employment Exchange** at least once a week, to register as looking for work ('sign on') and to collect your money – some casual workers, dock workers for example, had to sign on twice a day. All those not on NI benefit had to go through the degrading means test to prove they were poor enough for the dole. A benefit officer visited their home to find out what they possessed (if they had anything they could sell, for example). They also wanted to be told about any savings people had and any money other people in the house might have – for example, an elderly parent might have a pension or children might be earning. If their children earned even a few pence, their dole was reduced.

A British Medical Association study in 1933 showed it cost 5s 1d to feed a person the minimum of food for proper nourishment. By 1938 prices had risen and studies showed that 44% of those getting dole had to manage on less than this.

But in some ways, every unemployed person had a different experience. Were you willing to take any work, or just work at your trade? Would you spend day after day looking for work or did you, sometimes only after years of trying, give up? Did you have a family; if so, how big was it? Was your wife good at 'managing', or not? Were you happy to spend all your money on essentials – or did you spend it on beer and cigarettes? Many people joined savings clubs for necessities. They paid in a regular amount each week and then, when there was enough saved, bought the goods.

Source A — *From* The Road to Wigan Pier, *written by George Orwell in 1937. Orwell was a famous writer.*

Enormous groups of people, probably at least a third of the population of the industrial areas, live on the dole. The Means Test is very strictly enforced: you are refused **relief** at the slightest hint that you are getting money from another source. Dock-labourers, for instance, who are generally hired by the half-day, have to sign on at a Labour Exchange twice daily; if they fail to do so, it is assumed they have been working and their dole is reduced correspondingly…The most cruel and evil effect of the Means Test is the way in which it breaks up families. An old age pensioner, for instance, if a widower, would normally live with one or other of his children; his weekly ten shillings goes towards the household expenses…Under the Means Test, however, he counts as a 'lodger' and if he stays at home his children's dole will be docked.

Source B — *From a radio interview with Mrs Pallas in 1934.*

My husband has worked one year out of the last twelve and a half. His face was lovely when I married him, but now he's skin and bones. When I married he was healthy and had a good job earning £8–10 as a ship's riveter. He lost his job about four months after we married, so I've hardly known what a working wage was. We've stayed respectable, we don't waste nothing. Everything's patched and mended in our house. But there's no money for enjoyment – no going to the cinema, newspapers or going to the football.

Alfred Smith and his family

On 21 January 1939, the weekly magazine *Picture Post* had an article about Alfred Smith – just one of the 1,800,000 unemployed. Smith lived in Peckham, in South London. He was married, with four children. They lived in four rooms (one a very small kitchen) in the basement of a house. Smith had been out of work for three years. Three mornings a week he signed on at the Peckham Employment Exchange. He spent the rest of the time looking for work. This is how the article described Smith:

His face is lined, and his cheeks are sunken, because he has no teeth. He is only 35 years old. He walks with his hands in his pockets, shoulders bent, head slightly forward. And he looks down as he walks – the typical walk of the unemployed man. He has kept his spirits through three long years of disappointment. But he is beginning to feel that perhaps there is no longer a place for him in our scheme of things – that he must change or perish.

The Smiths' budget

The Smiths got 47s 6d a week. This is their weekly budget.

	s	d
Rent	14	6
Clothing club	6	0
Insurance	1	8
Coal club	2	0
Coke (fuel)	1	0
Light	6	0
Food	16	0
Total	**50**	**2**

Old money

12 pennies (d) = 1 shilling (s)

20s = £1 (one pound)

Source C	The Smith family sit down to dinner. Photograph from a follow-up article in Picture Post *about the Smiths, saying that, thanks to the article in January, Mr Smith now had a job digging ditches for air raid shelters.*

Activities

1 Compare Sources A and B.

   a Write a sentence or two saying which source best shows how unemployment affected family life.

   b Explain why you chose it.

   c Write a sentence explaining what you would use the other source to show and why.

2 What would you use the information of the Smith family to show and why?

'The town that was murdered'

> ## Learning objectives
>
> In this chapter you will learn about:
> - the reasons for the Jarrow Crusade, how it was organised and opposition to it
> - making inferences from sources.

Shipbuilding in the 1930s

Shipbuilding workers suffered high levels of unemployment in the 1930s. In 1930, shipyard owners set up the National Shipbuilders' Security Ltd (NSS) to 'rationalise' the industry, making it more efficient. In practice, this meant buying up shipyards, closing them and selling off, or renting, the land. The shipbuilding areas of the north east were **eligible** for help under the *Special Areas Act* of 1934. But this help only reached some areas.

Jarrow

Jarrow is in Tyneside and was part of the Special Area of the north east. However, the amount of money allowed in the *Special Areas Act* of 1934 was far too little. In 1936, there were regular debates in parliament about the need for more funding. They also debated the problems of deciding where and how money was to be raised and spent and how industries could be encouraged to move to these areas.

In 1936, parliament discussed the towns and cities where they gave government work 'as far as circumstances permitted'. About half of the places listed were in special areas: 40 in Scotland, 43 in Wales, 12 in the north west and 47 in the north east (including Jarrow). However, Jarrow was never given a government contract – there was no industry there to apply for it.

Almost all the workers in Jarrow, near Newcastle Upon Tyne, worked at Palmer's Shipyard. In 1934, the NSS closed Palmers. By 1935, unemployment in Jarrow was 64%. It improved in 1936, but by then people had been hungry for a long time – many were starving.

A march of their own

In 1936, the National Unemployed Workers' Movement organised a National Hunger March to London. People in Jarrow decided to hold their own march to ask for work for Jarrow. The NUWM did not want this – they wanted the unemployed to act together. The Labour Party supported the NUWM. But many people in Jarrow thought the government would be more likely to help if they did not march with the NUWM. Many officials and members of the NUWM were also communists; and their marches were seen as political. The members of Jarrow town council, from all political parties, planned the march and marched together for some of it. They chose 200 of the fittest of Jarrow's unemployed men to march – to underline that they wanted work and were fit for it, as well as to make sure they cope with the march itself. They took a petition signed by over a thousand people asking the government to provide work.

The march was called the Jarrow Crusade, not a hunger march. The aim was to give the march more respectability, so the banners were made of black and white cloth, not the usual red. The evening before they set off, there was a religious service and the Bishop of Durham blessed the march.

Source A	Unemployment in Jarrow 1929–36. There were about 9500 people in the workforce as a whole.		
1929	3245	**1933**	7170
1930	3643	**1934**	6462
1931	6603	**1935**	6053
1932	6793	**1936**	4065

Source B *From a 1996 interview with Bill Batty who grew up in Jarrow and was one of the marchers.*

There was real starvation on Tyneside. It was hard for my parents – I was one of ten children. I went to school in my bare feet with big holes in my trousers. In hot or cold, in winter with six inches of snow, I'd get home and my mother had to rub a towel on my feet to stop me getting frostbite. People can't believe this, but it's true. Even when Jarrow was busy, unemployment was still high. I was one of the few to get an apprenticeship in the shipyard and one of the last apprentices to come out of the yard before it closed. I cried when the cranes came down.

Source C *From The Town That was Murdered, written by Ellen Wilkinson, Labour MP for Jarrow, in 1939.*

In the early summer of 1934, it was announced that Palmer's Shipyard had been sold to the NSS. The death warrant of Palmer's was signed. The reason for Jarrow's existence vanished overnight.

73% of all those unemployed in Jarrow had been out of work for so long they no longer qualified for unemployment benefit. 43% of them had been out of work for a year – hundreds of men had had no work for five years. There was no work. No one had a job except a few railwaymen, officials, shop workers, and a few workmen who went out of the town. The plain fact is that if people have to live and bring up their children in bad houses on too little food, their resistance to disease is lowered. They die before they should.

Source D *A photograph of the Jarrow Crusade setting off. Only men were allowed to march. The woman, Emily Robb, and her children left the march on the outskirts of Jarrow.*

Activity

In pairs, write a two-minute radio broadcast from Jarrow as the march sets out. Use Sources A–D to help you give the listeners an idea of:

- why the marchers are going to London
- who marched
- how the march was organised
- what made it different from other hunger marches
- what it was like when they set out (radio listeners can't see the picture).

Marching to London

Learning objectives

In this chapter you will learn about:

● the marchers; their effect on public opinion
● considering the purpose of a source
● evaluating the utility or reliability of sources.

The marchers covered 291 miles in 22 stages. They had an old bus to carry their cooking equipment and sent people ahead to fix a place to stay and organise the cooking. They marched up to 21 miles between stops, often stopping for more than a day, so they could hold **public meetings** to explain what had happened in Jarrow and that they were asking for work, not benefits or charity.

Public reaction to the marchers varied. In some towns, the local cinemas let them in free; in Barnsley they used the **public baths** for free. Sometimes local church or council groups gave them tea and food at their stops. Sometimes they slept in halls, schools or churches; at other times they had to sleep in the **workhouse** – the last resort of the homeless and jobless.

Source A	*Part of a speech given by the Mayor of Jarrow when the marchers stopped in Ripon.*

In every town and city and village on the way to London we are going to put before the people the plight of our distressed town, so that public opinion may make itself felt. We don't want our people to be fed by charity. All we are asking is that our unemployed men be allowed to work and earn enough money to feed their wives and children.

Source B	*Bob Maugham, a marcher who had only had one month of work in ten years, remembering the meal in Leeds 60 years later.*

We got a grand meal in Leeds. Roast beef (we hadn't had that in a long time), Yorkshire pudding and a bottle of beer. Even in the Tory places we were mostly well looked after.

Source C	*The marchers being fed at a stop in Lavendon, between Bedford and Northampton.*

 ResultsPlus
Top Tip

Students considering the purpose of a source do well if they use the information in the caption to work out as much as possible about where the source comes from. A private diary has a different purpose from a newspaper interview. The same person may say different things about the same issue privately and publicly.

Source D *Part of a speech given to the marchers by the Reverend Thomas at Northallerton. The town council had not sent anyone to greet them.*

I don't think the decision of the council not to welcome the marchers represents the feeling of the people of Northallerton. This march is the finest organised I have ever seen. It is our duty to spare no effort to help our unfortunate comrades and I think the churches of this country should have led the march and taken it right to London as an appeal not only to the Government but also to the common humanity in man.

Source E *A painting of the Jarrow March, painted by art student Colin Moss in 1936. Moss came from a working-class background and believed in social reform. How might this have affected his painting?*

Source F *From a book about the Jarrow Crusade written in 2005.*

Regular donations to march funds showed the level of support for the Crusade. Donations came from passing motorists, from audiences at their daily public meeting, from workplace collections and from the general public. In total the Jarrow crusade raised £1,567 0s and 5d. Of this, £680 16s 11d came from the general public. A finance committee was in charge of keeping an account of all that was taken in and spent. In all, there were four committees organising the march: roads and food; finance; publicity; and health.

ResultsPlus
Build Better Answers

Exam question: How useful are Sources B and F as evidence of public reaction to the Jarrow Crusade? (10 marks)

■ **A basic answer (level 1)** only gives generalised answers, not giving details from the source or only considering who produced the source (for example, *Source B is useful because the person was on the march*).

● **A good answer (level 2)** gives examples of what the content of the sources is useful for or what we cannot find out from them (for example, *Source F is useful for public support, it tells you about the money given by the public*).

▲ **A better answer (level 3)** does both of the above.

▲ **An excellent answer (top of level 3)** considers all of the above and also thinks about how reliable the source is **or** the degree of support given (for example, *Source B is from a man who was on the march and saw the public reaction. But he gave this interview 60 years later. Maybe the good bits stuck in his mind while he tried to forget about the rain and when people were less kind*).

Activities

1 Was the painter of Source E in favour of the Jarrow Crusade, against it or neutral to it? Write a sentence explaining your view, with examples from the painting.

2 **a** In groups, make an index card for each source. Say what it is, where it comes from and who produced it. (If it is not possible to answer all these points, write 'can't tell'.)

 b Divide the cards up according to how useful the source is in showing the following aspects of the Jarrow March:

 • the feelings of the marchers
 • the organisation of the marchers
 • reasons for marching
 • support for the marchers.

The impact of the Jarrow Crusade

> **Learning objectives**
>
> In this chapter you will learn about:
> - the effects of the Jarrow Crusade
> - evaluating a hypothesis.

Government reaction

The Jarrow Crusade reached London on Saturday 31 October. Stanley Baldwin refused to see Ellen Wilkinson and accept the petition. While the march was in progress the **cabinet** (the most senior members of the government) had issued a statement disapproving of all marches, 'whatever their particular purpose'. The government made sure the marchers' benefit payments were stopped while they were on the march (leaving their families worse off than ever), because they were 'not available for work'. The Jarrow Unemployment Board offered work to one marcher, Samuel Anderson, at a shipyard near Jarrow to tempt him from the march. He didn't go. Parliament accepted the petition, but did not debate it.

Gains from the march?

There were some small gains. Several marchers were offered work but it meant leaving Jarrow. All but one marcher (whose sister lived in London where he was offered work as a baker) reluctantly refused. Sir John Jarvis, MP, had taken an interest in Jarrow. After the march, he said he would set up a steel works in Jarrow. His works opened in December 1937. It only employed 200 men and gave the government an excuse to ignore Jarrow.

The Jarrow legacy

Many of the marchers felt, and said, that the Crusade had failed. It did not achieve its aim. The government did not act, at once, to bring work to Jarrow. As the country rearmed in readiness for the Second World War, unemployment did drop and many Jarrow marchers found work. More than this, the Crusade became a legend, a byword for a public protest – a protest with huge public support. Support was less universal than people now believe. The political unity of the marchers did not last long either. The various political parties that came together for the march were soon opponents again. But the spirit of the marchers inspired many more modern protests.

Source A	A Labour Party election poster from the 1951 general election. Think about how the party is presenting itself in relation to the Jarrow Crusade.

Source B	A marcher's view, reported in the Star newspaper for 31 October 1936.

> The first morning is what I'm afraid of. It'll be getting up and looking out of the window at the same old sight – Jarrow, knowing there's nothing, nothing to do. My feet hurt terribly, but, all the same, it's been a holiday. While you're marching you don't think.

Source C — *From a debate in parliament about unemployment in Jarrow and the north east in 1986. Protesters had just staged another 'Jarrow March'. The speaker was Don Dixon, MP for Jarrow.*

I vividly recall the 1936 march. As a boy of seven, I saw the marchers leave. I asked my father why they were marching. He said they were going to London to find work. I asked: 'Would it not be easier to fetch the work up here where the men are?' That same question could be asked today – fifty years later.

Last night I presented a petition on behalf of people in my constituency. There is intolerably high unemployment in Jarrow, like many other constituencies in the north, the north west, Wales and Scotland. The Government's policies are turning our areas into industrial deserts. The Government has cut regional aid. Regional aid is not charity; we do not want charity. Regional aid is a right. Central government has to care for the regions. In Jarrow, long-term unemployment has risen from 900 to 3600. I recently had a letter from a constituent, who said: 'I am still unemployed after six years. I have filled in thousands of application forms and been on hundreds of job interviews. It is slowly driving me mad.'

Source D — *From a book about the Jarrow Crusade written in 2005.*

The struggles of the 1930s had an effect on rebuilding after the war. There was unemployment provision, a regional policy, the National Health Service and government commitment to full employment.

Source E — *A cartoon about a lorry drivers' slow drive from the north east to London to protest at rising fuel prices in November 2000.*

YEAH, IT'LL BE JUST LIKE THE JARROW HUNGER MARCH!

TYNESIDE-LONDON SLOW CONVOY

Activities

'The marchers might just as well have not have gone on the Jarrow Crusade. They didn't get much from it and their families lost benefit while they were away.'

1 In groups, divide the sources between you. Think about how far they support the statement above.

- Draw a scale line that runs from 'no support' on the left to 'complete support' on the right. Decide where to put each source on this scale and mark its letter on the scale.
- List the evidence from the source for your opinion.

2 Hold a debate about the statement, using the evidence from the sources and your own knowledge.

Know Zone
Unit 3B - Key Topic 1

In the Unit 3 exam, you will be required to answer five questions. You have only 1 hour and 15 minutes to answer these questions, so the examiners are not expecting you to write huge amounts. The number of marks given in the answer book help you judge how much to write. The time allocation to the right gives a little thinking time before you put pen to paper and a few minutes to read through your answers at the end.

Question 1: 10 minutes
Question 2: 12 minutes
Question 3: 12 minutes
Question 4: 12 minutes
Question 5: 20 minutes

We are going to look at Questions 1 and 2. The examples of Questions 1 and 2 on these pages are based on the chapter in Key Topic 1 called 'The Impact of the Jarrow Crusade' (on pages 20–21). In the examination, the sources will be provided in a booklet.

Results**Plus**
Maximise your marks

Question 1

Examiner's tip: Question 1 will ask you what you can learn about a particular topic from the sources provided. Be careful not to just copy information from the source. You need to make inferences from the sources – work something out based on the information in them. Let's look at an example (Source C on page 21).

'What can you learn from Source C about the impact of the Jarrow Crusade?' (6 marks)

Student answer	**Examiner comment**
The source tells me that the MP making the speech saw the Jarrow Crusade as a boy and remembers it.	This answer mainly reproduces information from the source and would get very few marks.

Let's rewrite the answer, making inferences and showing how the source helped us make them.

The source tells me that the MP making the speech saw the march as a boy and remembers it. So it must have made an impression on him. Moreover, it suggests the Jarrow Crusade had enough of an impact to be well known – he doesn't have to explain what it was to people and he's speaking in parliament, not in Jarrow.	In this answer there are two inferences made from the source (shown underlined), using detail from the source to support the inferences (shown in bold). This answer would get level 3. Two more supported inferences would get full marks. The important thing is to make valid inferences from the source and refer to the source to show how you made those inferences. However, marks are often lost at the end of an examination by spending too much time on the first question. Make sure not to spend more than 10 minutes reading, thinking and writing your answer. Three supported inferences are enough to get you full marks.

Question 2

Examiner's tip: This will be a question that asks about the purpose of a particular source. You need to think about the message of the source: what is it trying to say? This is not the same as the purpose of the source, but it helps you think about the purpose: what effect does the person who produced the source want to achieve? You should use your own knowledge of the historical context – what was happening at the time – to help you explain what the author was trying to achieve. Let's look at an example (Source E on page 21).

Study Source E and use your own knowledge. Why do you think a newspaper printed this cartoon? Use details from the cartoon and your own knowledge to explain your answer. (8 marks)

Student answer

The cartoon is showing modern truck drivers who went on a protest drive from Jarrow to London comparing themselves to the marchers, but the cartoonist thinks they have had a far easier time – going by truck instead of walking all the way. He also doesn't think they are starving as they are eating fast food.

Examiner comment

This answer goes beyond just describing the source in detail. It discusses a valid message for the source. But it does not discuss the purpose – why was the newspaper publishing that cartoon? So it would be marked at level 2.

Let's rewrite the answer, making the purpose and the message of the cartoon clear and putting it in context with our own knowledge (parts in **bold**).

The cartoon is showing modern truck drivers who went on a protest drive from Jarrow to London comparing themselves to the marchers, but the **cartoonist's message is that** they have had a far easier time – going by truck instead of walking all the way. Also, we know the marchers were not fat and overfed like these drivers and they didn't have fast food, either. **So, the newspaper must have printed the cartoon to make people compare** these protesters to the Jarrow marchers and think that they are not in nearly as much distress as the Jarrow marchers were so they should not be comparing themselves to those marchers (which they are in the cartoon).

Here, the message and the purpose of the source are clearly defined and the context is clear. This takes it to level 3.

Key Topic 2: Britain alone

On 3 September 1939, Britain and France declared war on Germany. They expected an immediate attack, but Germany, which had started the war by invading Poland, wanted complete control of Poland before moving into Western Europe. The attack on Europe began suddenly on 10 May 1940 and used a new tactic, *Blitzkrieg* ('lightning war'), to push rapidly though Luxembourg, Belgium and the Netherlands. The German army was moving rapidly across France in a matter of days. On 22 June 1940, France surrendered to the Germans. Britain was alone.

In this Key Topic, you will study:

○ the BEF, Dunkirk and Churchill
○ the Battle of Britain
○ the Blitz.

This book focuses on just one part of a wider world war – the war in Europe as it affected Britain. You will see how Britain and France were unprepared for Germany's *Blitzkrieg* attack, how France fell and the British were forced to evacuate from Dunkirk. You will consider Churchill's role as Britain stood alone. Churchill was made prime minister on 10 May 1940, and his speeches were seen at the time as vital in keeping morale up. You will also study the preparations for war and the effect of the German bombing of British cities, which brought the war to civilians who were far away from the fighting in a way that had never happened in war before.

Going to war

On 1 September 1939, the German army invaded Poland. Britain and France had been trying to avoid war with Germany by accepting Germany's breaking of the **Treaty of Versailles**, and its invasion of Czechoslovakia. This policy was known as appeasement. When Germany invaded Poland it became clear appeasement was not working, so Britain and France declared war on Germany. They expected Germany to invade France over the French–German border. As soon as war broke out, the British Expeditionary Force (BEF) was sent to France. By May 1940, it had 394,165 troops defending this border. But when the German attack came, it surprised them by its speed and direction: through Luxembourg, the Netherlands and Belgium. The BEF tried to counterattack, but the direction and speed of the German attack forced it to retreat.

Winston Churchill

Winston Churchill was an MP who had constantly criticised the government's appeasement policy before the war. When war broke out, Churchill was put in charge of the navy. On 10 May 1940, when the German invasion began, he was made prime minister. He was prime minister all through the war and had a great ability to inspire people to keep going in the fight against Germany, which was particularly important once France fell.

Source A — From Churchill, *written by Martin Gilbert in 1967.*

Churchill was Britain's war leader for five years. During the first year, Britain stood utterly alone after Hitler conquered Poland, Norway, Denmark, the Netherlands and France. It was at this desperate time that Churchill raised the spirit of the British people, rallied the downhearted, gave courage to those who were afraid and persuaded the whole nation that it should resist Germany to the end, even if the end were bitter.

Examination question

What was the purpose of this poster (Source B)? Use details of the poster and your own knowledge to answer this question. **(8 marks)**

Source B — *A poster issued by the British government in late 1940. The prime minister, Winston Churchill, stands in front of tanks and fighter planes. Think about the message the poster is trying to convey.*

"LET US GO FORWARD TOGETHER"

Blitzkrieg!

> ## Learning objectives
>
> In this chapter you will learn about:
>
> - the German invasion of the Netherlands, Belgium and France and the retreat of the BEF
> - making inferences from sources.

On 9 April 1940, Germany invaded Norway and Denmark, both neutral countries, without declaring war first. On 10 May, it launched Operation Yellow, the invasion of Western Europe. Germany's *Blitzkrieg* through Europe was a new military tactic. It followed this pattern:

- German planes bombed the area to be occupied.
- German tanks moved in and took over the area.
- German troops moved in and occupied the area, under cover of **artillery** fire.
- The planes and tanks moved on to the next target, leaving the troops to occupy the captured area and put down all resistance.

It was very risky to move into enemy territory without making sure the area behind the advancing army was safe. But it gave troops in the countries under attack little time to prepare for invasion. It was unexpected, terrifying and very effective. Belgian, British and then French troops were thrown into confusion. They tried to hold back the Germans, but had no plan, while the Germans had a very clear one. The BEF and other Allied troops were forced to retreat to **evacuate** from the French port of Dunkirk.

Source A	*From an interview with Agnis van Loon, about the invasion of Bergen op Zoom, the Netherlands in May 1940.*

About 40 of us hid in the cellar. There was the shock of hearing German commands, heavy boots and running. We heard shots and tried to see what was going on through the grille to the street above. The Germans gathered at the crossroads, lined up in rows and marched to the town centre. The deafening sound of those marching boots, the sound of their voices singing marching songs, had a chilling effect I will never forget.

Source B	A photo of a French village that has just been captured by the Germans. The photo is from Signal, a German **propaganda** magazine.

Results Plus

Top Tip

When asked how far sources support a statement, or agree with another source, students who do well will always think about both support (or agreement) and the lack of it.

Source C *The effects of Blitzkrieg, 1939–40.*

Key:
- Land occupied by the Soviet Union
- Land occupied by Germany
- Neutral countries
- German satellites
- → Allied troops evacuated
- → German invasion

Source D *From the letters and diaries of Christopher Seton-Watson, of the BEF. His company arrived in France on 5 December. Between 10 and 30 May, the company moved from France into Belgium and back to Dunkirk.*

10 May: Near Alost, we halted. There was a drone in the air, growing louder: 27 planes appeared, zig-zagging, looking for a target. We hid in the house shadows, a queer feeling in our stomachs. They passed and there were thuds not far behind us as they began bombing.

11 May: Bombing all day, waves of planes. All night the Belgian army retreated past the bombed house we slept in.

14 May: At dusk, a huge outbreak of firing told us our men were fighting German troops. We moved north – difficult over damaged roads jammed with **refugees**.

16–17 May: Much confusion with orders, but at 16:00 we were ordered to move back. It was a nightmare round Brussels. Allied army trucks and civilian vehicles kept breaking into our line. Many of our drivers had been going for so long they were falling asleep at the wheel.

27 May: At dawn, fighting with advancing German tanks, motorcycles, troop vehicles and later infantry on foot. Eventually had to pull out when came under fire from over 200 German infantry.

27

ResultsPlus
Build Better Answers

Exam question: What can you learn from Source D about the effects of *Blitzkrieg*? **(6 marks)**

When you are asked what you can learn from a source or sources, you are expected to make *inferences*. This means you work something out from the information in the source; you don't just copy it.

■ **A basic answer (level 1)** just repeats information from the source (for example, *it tells me that there was bombing, waves of planes and the soldiers ending up fighting the German army.*)

● **A good answer (level 2)** makes unsupported inferences from the source (for example, *it tells me that things were happening very fast, it was confusing and Blitzkrieg was frightening.*)

▲ **A better answer (level 3)** makes supported inferences from the source (for example, *it tells me that things were happening very fast in Blitzkrieg, because they are having to act before they get orders, it was confusing with all those refugees and the fleeing Belgian army.*)

Activity

Making an *inference* is working something out from information in a source. Read the inferences below about the effects of *Blitzkrieg*. Copy each inference and write next to it the letter(s) of the source(s) that you could make this inference from. You may be able to make more than one inference from a source.

- It caused a lot of damage.
- It scared people.
- It was very successful.

Dunkirk

> ## Learning objectives
>
> In this chapter you will learn about:
> - the importance of Dunkirk
> - Churchill and the reasons for British survival
> - considering the purpose of a source.

Operation Dynamo

On 21 May 1940, the first retreating Allied troops reached Dunkirk, the only French port not held by the Germans. Its long, shallow beach would be hard to evacuate from. The British navy made plans to rescue as many troops as possible before the Germans took Dunkirk. Operation Dynamo began on 26 May. The government asked owners of small boats to go to Dunkirk to ferry soldiers to the big ships. By 29 May, about 300 boats were doing this. The big boats shuttled from Dunkirk to Britain until 4 June. They had estimated 20,000–30,000 troops might be brought home. The final total was over 338,000 – a large part of the BEF and many Allied troops as well.

The importance of Dunkirk

Many people saw the evacuation of Dunkirk as a victory, even though Winston Churchill pointed out that 'wars are not won by evacuations'. However, the evacuation saved many soldiers who could fight again and it helped British morale. Churchill knew this was important. He feared France would fall and then Britain would be the only focus of the German army and its air force, the *Luftwaffe*. So despite his warning, he did his best to promote Dunkirk as an example of how the British people could work together to produce victory in the face of near certain defeat. 'Dunkirk spirit' became a phrase used for keeping going in the face of huge obstacles. When France did fall, the fact that the British had snatched so many troops from the overconfident Germans made people less likely to think Britain should just give in or that the Germans could never be beaten.

Source A *A painting of the last day of the evacuation of Dunkirk, commissioned by the War Artists' Advisory Committee soon after the event. The artist, Charles Crundall, was not at Dunkirk, but spoke to people who were. The details of the evacuation – the use of small ships to ferry troops, the troops massed on the beach and in the water, and the smoke of the burning oil tanks – are all accurate.*

Source B — *Christopher Seton-Watson was part of the BEF evacuated from Dunkirk.*

29 May: Dive-bombers came over again. Thick columns of black smoke rose from tankers burning in the harbour. Thousands of troops were waiting on the beach for orders. There seemed to be no organisation. Soldiers waded into the sea to be picked up by small boats. We decided to use the pier, where larger boats were picking up.

30 May: By 03:00, it was clear there was no hope of boarding until daylight. There was fog at first light and bombing, but the RAF kept the bombers away. There was enemy shelling, mostly at our pier. By now, embarkation was more organised. We were given number 69; 6 was just setting off. At 20:30, it was our turn and we raced through the shelling to HMS *Codrington*. We sailed at 21:30 with over a thousand aboard.

Source C — *Part of the speech made by Winston Churchill on 4 June 1940.*

The Royal Navy, helped by countless ordinary seamen, embarked the Allied troops; often in bad weather, under an almost ceaseless hail of bombs and artillery fire in seas full of submarines and mines. Our men carried on, with little or no rest, for days and nights on end; trip after trip across the dangerous waters.

Our thankfulness at this escape must not blind us to the fact that this was a military disaster. We must expect another blow almost at once. We shall fight in France, we shall fight on the seas and oceans, we shall fight in the air. We shall defend our Island, whatever the cost. We shall fight on the beaches, we shall fight on the landing grounds, we shall fight in the fields and in the streets. We shall never surrender.

Source D — *From the Naval Staff History of Operation Dynamo, written in 1947 using naval information from the evacuation. At first, only naval officers had access to these reports. This one was first published in 2000.*

Some delays occurred in the gathering of small craft at Ramsgate, as many had been sent to Dover in error. Once this happened, there was no way of communicating with them until they reached Dover. This resulted in delays of up to 24 hours or more before they gathered in Ramsgate. During the night, bad weather caused several collisions and vessels being cast adrift.

Examination question

What was the purpose of the illustration shown in Source A? Use details of the illustration and your own knowledge to answer the question. (8 marks)

Activities

1. Source A was put on display in the National Gallery as soon as it was finished. Write a newspaper report by a journalist who went to the unveiling. Consider:
   - why the War Artists' Advisory Committee wanted it painted and publicly displayed
   - what the painting seems to be saying about Dunkirk.

2. Turn Churchill's speech (Source C) into four simple sentences.

3. Show how Churchill uses the following to make his speech dramatic (give one example for each):
   - repetition
   - adjectives.

4. If the navy didn't want to make the information in Source D public, why did they have the report made at all?

The Battle of Britain

Learning objectives

In this chapter you will learn about:

● the Battle of Britain

● making inferences from sources.

When France surrendered on 22 June 1940, Hitler turned to Britain. Operation Sealion (the invasion of Britain) relied on destroying the Royal Air Force (RAF) so it could not attack invading troops. The British were equally determined to win air supremacy – if not, Britain would be at the mercy of the *Luftwaffe*, and might be bombed into defeat.

What was the Battle of Britain?

The Battle of Britain was not a single battle, or even a few battles. It was the battle between the RAF and the *Luftwaffe* for control of the air over Britain, and it was fought over many months.

There were four stages to the Battle of Britain:

● **10 July–7 August:** *Luftwaffe* attacks on the British coast, especially RAF radar stations

● **8 August–6 September:** *Luftwaffe* attacks on RAF airfields

● **7–15 September:** *Luftwaffe*, thinking RAF beaten, attack London

● **15 September:** *Luftwaffe* defeated. This is now Battle of Britain Day, because it convinced the *Luftwaffe* that the RAF was still a fighting force. On 17 September, Hitler called off Operation Sealion.

Some people see 17 September as the end of the Battle of Britain. Some say (because there was still fighting over Britain afterwards) that it ended on 31 October, when the *Luftwaffe*'s focus shifted to the Soviet Union.

Why did Britain win?

In July 1940, the RAF had 640 fighter planes. The German *Luftwaffe* had 2600 bombers and fighter planes within striking distance of Britain, in occupied Europe. They were convinced that the RAF would soon be wiped out. But the RAF had some advantages. Firstly, they had **radar**, a system invented in 1935 and installed all along the south and east coasts of Britain at the start of the war. Radar uses radio waves to detect moving objects that the waves bounce off. It could detect the *Luftwaffe* and warn the RAF of how many planes were coming and where they were heading. Also, while the Germans had the *Luftwaffe* and many more bomber planes, the RAF had more fighter planes and its Spitfire planes were the most efficient design. British factories worked around the clock to build more planes, and replaced lost planes much more quickly than the Germans did. Also, 'Dunkirk spirit' kept the RAF pilots flying, despite terrible losses. Once the Battle of Britain was won, Churchill said of those pilots, 'never in the field of human conflict was so much owed by so many to so few'.

Source A | *Frank Walker-Smith's flight report from his first flight on 18 August. His squadron of 13 planes fought 250 Luftwaffe planes.*

At 17:30, I was ordered up with my squadron. Enemy spotted east of Thames estuary. I picked out an Me110. After about one-and-a-half minutes of steep turning, I attacked front on from above it, opening fire at 100–150 yards above it. I saw smoke coming from both engines as it glided down to strike the sea. After giving other enemy aircraft short bursts I delivered another frontal attack on an Me110, which broke up at about 3000 feet. The rear gunner or pilot bailed out. This attack took place at 5000 feet, about 60 miles due east of Margate. Only one person bailed out. Enemy casualties: two Me110s destroyed.

ResultsPlus
Top Tip

When asked what they can learn from a source, students who do well will make an *inference* – they will work out the implications of what the source is saying and refer to the source to support it. So, for Source A one inference would be that they had good warning of the enemy coming: they were in the air and looking for them.

Key events of the Battle of Britain.

Date	Event
10 July 1940	*Luftwaffe* begins bombing attacks on British coast, especially radar stations.
12 August	*Luftwaffe* bombs British airfields and radar stations on the coast.
13 August	*Luftwaffe* bombs British airfields in Essex, Kent, Sussex and Hampshire, and aircraft factories.
15 August	*Luftwaffe* flies over 2000 raids. The day of heaviest fighting. Luftwaffe lost 75 planes, RAF lost 34.
16–18 August	Heavy fighting and losses.
7 September	*Luftwaffe* bombs London for the first time. The start of the Blitz.
7–15 September	*Luftwaffe* bombs London daily.
17 September	*Luftwaffe* runs one last bombing raid on airfields. They lost 60 planes (first reports put the loss as high as 185).

Source B — *From a book about Polish fighter pilots in Britain, written in 1998. It was Germany's invasion of Poland that started the war. Many Polish pilots escaped to fight from France and then, when France was captured, from Britain. The pilot in the extract, Boleslow Wlasnowolski, joined the RAF at Biggin Hill in early August 1940. His first flight was on 14 August.*

On 13 September, Wlasnowolski moved to No 607 Squadron at Tangmere, and two days later he shot a Do17Z down into the sea. On 17 September he was posted to No 213 Squadron (which was also based at Tangmere), where he claimed his last victory on 15 October. Wlasnowolski was killed on 1 November – the day he received a posting to a Polish fighter squadron – when he was shot down.

Source C — *A cartoon published in a British newspaper on 19 August 1940.*

"597–598–599–600..."

Activities

1   In groups, discuss what you can learn from the sources about pilots in the Battle of Britain.
    Source A has been done for you.

Source	A	B	C
It suggests…	they were well trained		
because…	he knew what to do when they met the enemy, pick one and fight it, and he knew how best to do that.		

2   Plan an information sheet about the Battle of Britain for Year 5 students using Sources A, B and C on these pages. You should write 200 words.

Preparing for war

> **Learning objectives**
>
> In this chapter you will learn about:
> - government preparation for attacks on Britain
> - making inferences from sources.

Preparing for bombing

Long before war began, the government prepared for war, certain that cities would be bombed. As early as 1935, it told local councils to build **air raid shelters**. The Air Raid Precautions (ARP) service was set up in 1937, with voluntary ARP wardens. By September 1939, there were over 1.5 million ARP wardens. The wardens put **sandbags** around buildings to stop bomb damage and put up huge **barrage balloons** to stop German planes flying low. They organised the '**blackout**': stopping lights showing after dark, which would show a bomber overhead that people were below. Streetlights were turned off. People covered their windows with cloth or paper. ARP wardens sounded the air raid siren to warn of an air raid, and the 'all-clear' when the raid was over. They checked that people went to shelters. Councils built a few shelters big enough to hold 50 people, but not many. The government decided not to crowd people together during bombing. Instead, from early 1939 onwards, they gave out Anderson Shelters – iron shelters to bolt together and bury in the garden.

When the bombing began, ARP wardens called the emergency services: Fire Brigade, Heavy Rescue Squads (who were trained to dig through the rubble to find survivors) and the Ambulance Service.

Preparing for invasion

On 14 May 1940, the war **minister**, Anthony Eden, asked for volunteers for a Local Defence Force (LDF). He expected about 150,000 volunteers; there were 250,000 on the first day. In August, the LDF, now about 1 million strong, was renamed the Home Guard. Because of the huge numbers, it took until the beginning of 1941 to give all the groups equipment and uniforms, but they began training straight away. The Home Guard manned anti-aircraft guns during air raids – the guns that tried to shoot down enemy planes. Over a thousand were killed on this duty during the war. They helped rescue workers after air raids, and cleared up the bomb damage, making roads clear first. They removed or painted over road and station signs, so the enemy would not know where they were if they landed in Britain. They put obstacles in large fields that might be used to land planes and they put barbed wire along the beaches. They were in charge of detonating or making-safe unexploded bombs. Most importantly, they trained to fight a German invasion.

Source A	From a diary kept by Pat Ashford for the project, Mass Observation. This project asked people to keep daily diaries of their lives to be used as a record of the times. Think why this kind of diary might be different from a personal one.

29 August 1939: On the way home, I bought a torch and battery and looked at stuff for blackout curtains for the dining room. It would cost at least £1 to darken. I think I'll wait and see what happens.
30 August 1939: On the way home, I bought another torch and battery. I had another look at the blackout material.
1 September 1939: Our blackout curtains are now up. The whole town seems to be buying blackout paper – about every sixth person has a roll. Buses and trams are running with only headlights and the barrage balloon is up.

> **Examination question**
>
> **What is the purpose of the poster (Source D)? Use details of the poster and your own knowledge to answer the question.**
>
> **(8 marks)**

Source B *From the Mass Observation diary of Eileen Potter, who lived and worked in London. At this point, there had been no serious bombing. How do you think too many nights like this would affect people?*

25 June 1940: Woke at 1 am to the air raid siren hooting. Jump out of bed and dress in old clothes by the bed ready. I run upstairs for cushions to take to the Anderson Shelter. By the time we are ready and crossing the garden to the shelter, Mr H, the ARP warden, is looking in the back gate to see if we are alright. We settle in the shelter with cushions and rugs. I suddenly realise I am very thirsty. Brenda [her sister] went to sleep in a corner. Jack F goes out to have a look round then and Mrs F [neighbours] can't settle. If anything destroys my morale, it will be being cooped up in this shelter with such fidgety people. Brenda brought some cards to the shelter, so we try to play by torchlight, but doesn't work very well. No sound of bombing. Even I go out to wander over to the H's shelter to see how they are getting on. In the end, Mr H is just saying we might as well go back when the 'all-clear' sounds. It is dawn – might as well get up.

Source C *From the Mass Observation diary of Edward Ward, who joined the Home Guard and was sent on several training courses.*

8 August 1940: What you are taught is not pretty. You learn how to stab a tank crew sentry in the back, so that he dies without making any noise. You are then told how to deal with the sleeping crew with nothing but a piece of lead pipe. We were told a lot about how to stop trains by filling the oil boxes with sand or grit. I learned a lot about street fighting and defending houses from a man who learned in the Spanish Civil War.

Source D *A government poster warning people to wait for their eyes to adjust before setting off in the blackout. There were many minor accidents (such as sprained ankles) in the first few weeks of the blackout.*

Activities

1 Making an *inference* is working something out from information in a source. Read the inferences below that can be made about preparations for war. Copy each inference and write next to it the letter(s) of the source(s) that you could make this inference from. You may be able to make more than one inference from a source.

- The precautions were dangerous.
- Some people obeyed the precautions.
- The precautions were a worry.
- The government was convinced there would be bombing and an invasion.

2 Write a sentence or two explaining what you can learn from the written sources that is not in the main information text on page 32. Give examples.

Evacuation

> ### Learning objectives
>
> In this chapter you will learn about:
> - the evacuation of the cities
> - evaluating a hypothesis.

At the start of the war, the government was so sure the Germans would bomb British cities, especially London, that they began evacuating people from London before declaring war. Most **evacuees** were children, but the government also evacuated some mothers of children under school age, pregnant women and blind people. This reduced the number of people in cities and it kept children (and other vulnerable groups), who would not be able to cope well with bombing, safe. It also freed parents and carers to work in volunteer groups such as the ARP or the WVS (Women's Voluntary Service).

From 1938 onwards, the government encouraged people to think about evacuation. Many people who could afford to do so made their own arrangements for evacuation with friends, family, or even strangers in the countryside.

But most ordinary children went, by train or bus, with their school. Schools practised evacuation procedure. On 1 September 1939, the evacuation began for real. In the first four days, 3 million people were evacuated, most of them children. By December, there had been no bombing. Many people went back for Christmas.

| Source B | *Written in 1987 by Beryl Heard, who was ten when she was evacuated from London in 1939.* |

> We were given a list of things to pack. Then we were given a departure date and it came and went. Then we were given another date, and never left London. My mother was fed up with packing and unpacking, so when we were told to be ready the third time she just put a few clothes in the case [to take to school]. But we went – with about half the things we needed.

| Source A | *A photo of an evacuation from London on 1 September 1939.* |

Source C | *From the Mass Observation diary of Eileen Potter, an evacuation officer for London County Council.*

1 September 1939: Arrived at East Acton station at 7:15. The station closed to the public at about 8:15. Children from the nearest school began to arrive well before then. They marched up, all carrying kit and gas masks. Some parents came to see them off; had to say goodbye at the entrance, no room on the platform. Hardly any tears, there is a general feeling they will be back next week.

3 September 1939: Early in the afternoon had to go to Guildford with an emergency evacuation. Met up with a collection of mothers, babies and unattached children. I marched them off to the underground, helped by a 12-year-old boy who said, 'We must all pull together in these times, mustn't we, Miss?' A father, seeing my LCC armband, put two small boys in my care, saying their mother will be down tomorrow.

Source D | *From a history of evacuation in World War Two.*

Getting the children out of London worked surprisingly well. The problems came on arrival. The government had left arrangements for the children's arrival and care to local authorities, telling them to do their best. The result was as a typically British wartime shamble. Hundreds of children arrived in the wrong place with not enough rations. More worryingly, there were not enough homes to put them in. A year before, the government had made lists of willing homes, but did not consider how many better-off families would make their own plans. When the trains arrived, many people on the list already had evacuees by private arrangement.

Source E | *From the Mass Observation diary of Tilly Rice, pregnant mother of two, who lived near London. Tilly and the children stayed on at a Cornish home the family had rented for an August holiday.*

5 December 1939: From everywhere I hear of people returning home. We have not yet decided what to do. It seems to me that they should have thought more about evacuation. The psychological effects may well be as bad as living in wartime conditions. All that money spent on evacuation could have been spent on making schools safe and building good air raid shelters.

6 February 1940: Travelled home. Everyone is still carrying out their air raid duties here, very good of them, considering nothing has happened now for five months.

ResultsPlus
Build Better Answers

Exam question: 'The 1939 evacuation of London was well organised.' How far do the sources support this statement? (16 marks)

In Question 5, when asked how far sources support a statement, it is important to produce a balanced judgment about how far the sources support the statement, using detail from the sources.

■ **A basic answer (level 1)** makes a generalised comment (for example, *Yes, it shows the children brought their things with them*).

● **A good answer (level 2)** makes a judgment about the statement, referring to the sources, but not in detail and not at length (for example, *Source A makes them look very organised. They have their cases and labels and sound really organised in Source C as well. But then B suggests that it was a shambles, because they got sent for over and over and then went without half of their things.*

▲ **A better answer (level 3)** develops a level 2 answer, usually deciding on either support or the lack of it. *Sources A and C make it seem organised and calm. Source D suggests the problems were at the other end – supporting the picture of an organised evacuation in A and C. Source B doesn't support it at all – they get sent for and then back and in the end do go, but are hardly expecting to and only have half their things. Their evacuation could have been the only one messed about – you'd need more evidence to be sure. The weight of the evidence, from the time and after, seems to support the statement.*

▲ **An excellent answer (level 4)** considers the extent of support, showing both support and the lack of it, with clear examples from the sources. It then delivers a balanced answer, taking into account the reliability of the sources.

Activity

In groups, prepare to debate how far the sources support the statement below. Use all the sources and your own knowledge.

'The evacuation at the start of the war was disruptive and unnecessary.'

Blitz

> **Learning objectives**
>
> In this chapter you will learn about:
> - the Blitz and its effects generally
> - evaluating the utility or reliability of sources.

The **Blitz** is the name given to the bombing of British cities by the *Luftwaffe* from 7 September 1940 to May 1941. It overlapped with the Battle of Britain (see pages 30–31). London was bombed first, most often and most heavily – it was bombed for 75 out of the first 76 nights of bombing (one night it was too foggy to fly). There were bombing raids on many other British cities, for example Coventry and Liverpool. The *Luftwaffe* targeted Liverpool as the most likely destination for US ships bringing supplies to Britain.

The Blitz was different from all previous bombing raids. The first bombs dropped on London were dropped on the industrial East End but, mostly, the raids deliberately targeted civilians, not military or industrial targets. The Germans wanted to disrupt daily life and kill many civilians. They wanted to wreck British morale, so that the public no longer supported the war.

Did it work?

The Blitz certainly disrupted life in the bombed cities. Over 43,000 civilians were killed and over 2 million people were made homeless by the bombing (estimates of these numbers vary widely). Water, gas and electricity supplies were affected. At best, all people lost was a lot of sleep. A survey of Londoners showed that on 12 September 1940, 32% of people got less than 4 hours sleep; 31% got none at all. This went on night after night, which must have severely affected people's lives. There was also a second evacuation; families were broken up, some for a second time. But the Blitz failed in its main objective. People did not turn against the war in large numbers.

Source A	*From an article for the US* New Yorker *magazine, written by Mollie Panter-Downes, an American who lived in London during the war.*

14 September 1940
Hardly anyone has slept at all in the past week. The *Blitzkrieg* continues to be directed against such military objectives as the tired shop girl, the red-eyed clerk, and the thousands of weary families patiently wheeling their few belongings in prams away from the wreckage of their homes. The amazing part of it is the cheerfulness and strength with which people do their jobs under nerve-wracking conditions. Girls have taken twice as long to get to work and look worn when they arrive, but their faces are nicely made up and they bring you a cup of tea or sell you a hat as chirpily as ever.

ResultsPlus
Top Tip

When asked about how useful a source is for a particular purpose, students need to do more than give a general comment about its usefulness (for example, *because the person was there at the time*). They need to consider how useful the source is for the particular purpose, using detail from the source. They also need to consider how typical or reliable the sources are.

Source B — *From the Mass Observation diary of Christopher Tomalin, a 28-year-old who lived with his parents in London, 15 September 1940.*

We can't afford to buy stuff for a 'refuge room'. We have no Anderson Shelter. We must use the pantry under the stairs: one wall is an outside wall; the other is thin board. I am scared by the indiscriminate night bombing of London and the rest of England. It is obvious the RAF and the anti-aircraft people can't do much about it. We can beat them in daylight, but not when it's dark. How can I, or anyone, sleep under these conditions?

Source C — *From the Mass Observation diary of Pam Ashford, who lived in London, 15 September 1940.*

Earlier this week, I said that people did not seem to be taking the idea of invasion seriously enough. They do now. No one doubts that we'll win. The sooner they come, the sooner they will be defeated. Hatred against the Germans is now intense – parachutists and seaborne invaders would get badly beaten up.

Source D — *A photo taken during the Blitz on London. Not many colour photos were taken at the time, as the film and processing was difficult and expensive.*

Activities

1 On an index card write down which source you think best shows the effects of the Blitz and explain why you chose it.

2 Now do the same for the source you think the Nazis would want to use in 1940 to show public reaction to the Blitz.

3 Now do the same for the source you think the British government would want to use in 1940 to show public reaction to the Blitz.

Blitz on Coventry

Learning objectives

In this chapter you will learn about:

- the Blitz on Coventry
- considering the purpose of a source.

After the London Blitz, the RAF bombed German cities too. Civilians on both sides were 'getting it' – as the British often referred to the bombing. On 8 November 1940, the RAF bombed Munich. The *Luftwaffe* bombed Coventry in retaliation, in a raid so destructive that a new word came into use: 'coventration' – wiping something out completely.

The bombing began at 7:20 pm on 14 November. Bombs were dropped in the city centre to start fires to guide later bombers. Hours later, the city was burning so fiercely that it was visible from 150 miles away. The bombing went on all night – 500 bombers dropped thousands of bombs. The 'all-clear' did not go until 6:15 the next morning. Estimates of those killed range from 380–554 and there were thousands of injuries. Over 4000 homes were destroyed as well as factories, businesses and the city's cathedral. The *Luftwaffe* returned to Coventry 40 times, the last raid being in August 1942. But the first raid was by far the worst.

Source B	*Ted Simmonds lived in Coventry, repairing various large machines for food preparation. This is part of an account compiled by his daughter from his hand-written recollections.*

The morning after the Blitz, council officials came to ask him for help. Thousands of homeless people were wandering the city. All gas and water mains were disrupted.

The most urgent need was to give people hot tea and maybe some bread. The officials had sent men to map the broken mains to find the best routes for repairs to the Technical College (the only large building still standing in the town centre) and the bakeries.

Could Ted suggest a way to provide a lot of hot water? And could he get some food preparation machinery into the College, so they could get on with more substantial supplies of emergency food?

Source A	*A photo of Coventry taken on 9 December 1940.*

Source C *Part of an article in the* Guardian *newspaper for 16 November 1940.*

The famous Cathedral is little more than a skeleton, masses of rubble piled inside its bare walls, while other targets included two hospitals, two churches, hotels, clubs, cinemas, public shelters, **public baths**, police station, and post office. The Mayor (Alderman J. A. Moseley) also gave the assurance that 'everything possible will be done for the sufferers and the homeless'. Mobile canteens are doing magnificent work in helping to feed the homeless people, and this evening private cars, loaded to capacity with comforts were pouring into the city. Within a few hours of the raid, Mr Herbert Morrison, Minister of Home Security, was on the scene. Mr Morrison said: 'The National Service units of the city have done their duty magnificently. They have shown great courage and determination under exceptional strain. I am very grateful to them for their devotion to duty. The local authority is taking full and prompt measures to deal with the emergency.'

Results Plus

Watch out!

When asked about the *purpose* of a source, do not confuse 'message' with 'purpose'. The purpose of a source is the effect the person who produced it wants it to have. The message of Source D could be 'we are coping'. The purpose of the photo was probably to raise morale.

Source D *A photo taken in Coventry after heavy bombing on 10 April 1941.*

Activities

1 In pairs, discuss why you think Source A was taken. Think of two good reasons for your answer.

2 In pairs, read Source C.

    a Write down four words or phrases you think show the writer wanted the reader to think well of the people of Coventry.

    b Write down a sentence you think shows the writer wanted the reader to think badly of the Germans.

    c Write a one-sentence slogan to convey the message of Source C.

    d Write a sentence describing its purpose.

New dangers

> ## Learning objectives
>
> In this chapter you will learn about:
> - how German bombing changed and developed after the Blitz
> - cross-referencing sources
> - considering the purpose of a source.

More bombing

The end of the Blitz ended the heavy bombing of those target cities; but the *Luftwaffe* still bombed Britain. There were many other raids – smaller, but still devastating for the bombed places. In April 1942, the Germans planned raids on new targets, smaller towns of no military importance. These are often called *Baedeker* raids because the Germans were said to have chosen their targets from towns with three stars in the German Baedeker tourist guide to Britain. The big Baedeker raids in April were on Exeter, Bath, York and Norwich. In June, the *Luftwaffe* bombed Canterbury after the RAF bombed Cologne. While the raids caused a lot of damage, the *Luftwaffe* suffered heavy losses. They had even heavier losses in the last big raids, in January 1943. They lost a bomber and four trained crew for every five civilians killed.

New bombs

So the Germans looked for ways to bomb Britain from a distance. German scientists had developed a flying bomb called *Vergeltung* ('retribution'), V1 for short. V1s were driven by a motor that was supposed to cut out over the target. They were launched from the French coast. The first V1s were launched on 12 June 1944. Over 9000 V1s were launched; many failed to reach their targets and some failed to explode. They killed about 6000 people, and did cause panic at first – about 1.5 million people left London. In September, the V2 was used. It was rocket-powered, so was faster and could go higher, although it only had the same amount of explosive, so caused no more damage than the V1 when it exploded. Over 5000 were launched, but only about 1000 reached Britain, killing about 2700 people.

Source A | *A cartoon published in a British newspaper on 19 June 1944. Think about the message of the cartoon and the purpose of the cartoonist in drawing it.*

"GOOD HEAVENS, WE CAN'T WIN A WAR THIS WAY!"

Source B | *From the Mass Observation diary of Maggie Joy Blunt, who lived in Slough, for 25 June 1944.*

The first day they came over, we were told to go to the shelters. I took one look at them and fled. N says they have had a demoralising effect in London – to hear them coming and not know where they will fall. There is no defensive gunfire as a warning. She says she prefers the ordinary Blitz and has had very little sleep recently. She has even sent me a copy of her will to keep safe. Have been told that there are only enough of these bombs to last a fortnight, but that then they will be replaced by some other Secret Weapon.

Source C — *Some 1944 entries from the Mass Observation diary of Edward Stebbing, who worked in a North London hospital.*

19 June: Talk about the pilotless planes is endless. It seems they travel too fast and too low for radar or the anti-aircraft guns to catch them. I must admit these things have put my nerves on edge more than ordinary raids. I suppose it is because they are new and so devilishly clever.

22 June: I went to look at the destruction caused by a P-plane that fell in Tottenham Court Road three days ago. I was surprised that the really bad damage seemed confined to quite a small area.

26 June: The baker told my landlady he didn't bake enough bread for everyone today – they had to keep stopping work for the flying bombs.

27 June: I heard one of the flying bombs for the first time last night – I hope it will be the last. It seemed to come low over the houses, making the house vibrate with the noise then the engine suddenly stopped and I thought our last hour had come.

Source D — *From the memories of Ivy Gross, interviewed about her wartime experiences in 1970.*

I never left London all through the war. In the Blitz, you had warning and time to get to shelters. I had the round of an insurance salesman who went off to fight. So I was out on my bike every day, visiting the people on my round, collecting money, having a cup of tea. We didn't like the V1s ('doodlebugs' we called them, because of the engine noise) because you knew if you could hear the engine cutting out the blast would be near you. I was blown off my bike once. But the V2s were the worst. You didn't hear them coming – just the bang as they exploded. I don't think we could have held out with them coming over for too many months.

Source E — *A photo taken after one of the last V2s hit Smithfield, London on 25 April, 1945. The government stopped the publication of the photo. Why do you think they did this?*

Activities

1   Write a paragraph explaining how far Sources B, C and D agree about the effect of the V1 and V2 bombs on morale.

2   Write a paragraph explaining how far Sources A and E agree about the effect of the V1 and V2 bombs on morale.

3   Write a sentence explaining the message of Source A.

4   Look at Source E.

   a   Write a note from the photographer to his newspaper, explaining why he took the photo.

   b   Write a note from the government to his newspaper, explaining why they can't print it.

Know Zone
Unit 3B - Key Topic 2

In the Unit 3 exam, you will be required to answer five questions: You have only one hour and 15 minutes to answer these questions, so the examiners are not expecting you to write huge amounts. The number of marks given in the answer book help you judge how much to write. The time allocation to the right gives a little thinking time before you put pen to paper and a few minutes to read through your answers at the end.

Question 1:	10 minutes
Question 2:	12 minutes
Question 3:	12 minutes
Question 4:	12 minutes
Question 5:	20 minutes

We are going to look at Question 3. We are going to focus on the chapter in Key Topic 2 called 'Blitz on Coventry' (pages 38–39).

ResultsPlus
Maximise your marks

Question 3

Examiner's tip: Question 3 will ask you to use three sources and consider the extent to which they say the same thing or support a statement. So the question tests cross-referencing sources.

In the exam, there are two slightly different question types used to test this skill. You might be asked 'Do these sources support the view that…?' or you could be asked 'How far do these sources agree about…? (10 marks). Whichever question is asked, the same mark scheme will be used. Let's look at an example (Sources A, B and C on pages 38–39). 'Do Sources A, B, and C support the view that the local response to the bombing of Coventry was well organised?' (10 marks)

Student answer

The sources show that the bombing was awful but the local authorities got on with dealing with it.

OR

I don't think that they show that. There were huge amounts of mess.

Examiner comment

These are two different level 1 answers. Level 1 answers decide that the sources either support or do not support the view under discussion and don't use information from the sources to back up what they say.

Let's see what we would have to do to reach level 2.

The sources show that the authorities were working hard. In Source B they are there on the first day trying to get hot drinks and food set up in the only building still standing in the city centre: that is working hard. Source C supports this with the mention of the mobile canteens feeding the homeless. In Source A the roads are pretty clear, so the local people have probably moved the rubble. **On the other hand, you could say that when you look at Source A there is no sign of the local authorities clearing things up and in Source C it praises the National groups and talks about private cars bringing 'comforts'…**

At level 2, the answers produce detail from specific sources as support (or lack of support) for the statement. To reach the top of the level, an answer would need to produce examples of both agreement and disagreement (**disagreement in bold**). But to reach level 3 an answer needs to consider how strongly the view is supported. So they need to consider how reliable the source is, perhaps, or how typical.

Let's look at a basic level 3 answer.

I think the sources provide some support, but possible evidence against this idea too. In Source A, they seem to have got the streets clear so people can go to work and so on, as the rubble would not have fallen so neatly. That suggests organisation, as does Source C when the minister who went down talked about them coping 'magnificently' and taking 'prompt' action. **You do have to wonder, though, if all the streets were as clear as the one shown in Source A – maybe this is the only street they have really sorted out.**

This answer considers the detail of the source and clearly cross-refers between sources. It also considers the typicality of Source A (**shown in bold**). But it does not consider the degree of support provided by all of the sources, which would lift it to full marks.

Let's see what we would have to do to get full marks.

I think the sources provide some support, but possible evidence against this idea too. In Source A, they seem to have got the streets clear so people can go to work and so on, as the rubble would not have fallen so neatly. That suggests organisation, as does Source C when the minister who went down talked about them coping 'magnificently' and taking 'prompt' action. But then, Source B suggests they were at a bit of a loss – they had to find Ted Simmonds and ask him what to do and how to get things working. You do have to wonder, though, if all the streets were as clear as the one shown in Source A – maybe this is the only street they have really sorted out.

It is always possible, too, that the author of Source B is overplaying how important they thought he was, to make him seem vital. With Source C, newspapers are supposed to report impartially, but they don't always, it was wartime and there was censorship and you certainly wouldn't expect a minister at the time to do anything but praise everyone, to keep morale up.

This answer would get full marks.

Key Topic 3: Britain at war

As the war continued, the government took an increasing role in everyday life. It controlled the flow of information, through censorship and propaganda. It also took control of food supplies and introduced the rationing of an increasing number of goods from petrol to clothing. The government also encouraged women to do war work, as they had in the First World War. The war was finally won with the help of the vast resources of the USA.

In this Key Topic, you will study:

- the role of the government, food supplies and rationing
- the changing role of women
- D-Day and the defeat of Germany.

You will see how the government worked to control morale and to keep the country running despite the disruption of war damage, dislocated families and restricted supplies of food and other essential goods. You will study how many women joined the armed forces and many more worked on the Home Front – often becoming independent for the first time. You will consider the 'drive to victory' at the end of the war and how, and why, Germany was finally defeated.

Government control

During the war, the government needed to keep much tighter control over the country than it had in peacetime. It needed much more central organisation to plan war production, **rationing** and evacuation. It needed to release a lot more public information on what to do in the **blackout**, what to do in an air raid, how to cope with rationing and how to help the war effort. It also needed to warn people about the dangers of talking too freely about things like troop movements or the consequences of wasting food.

Not everyone supported the war. Many pacifists spoke out against it. If they did so publicly, they were often arrested.

New ministries

As early as 1939, the government had set up a new **Ministry** of Supply that took over the iron and steel industry to organise the production of war supplies. Other industries, for example coal mining, also came under government control. Some existing ministries were given extra responsibilities – the Ministry of Labour became the Ministry of Labour and National Services (responsible for organising the armed services and the war effort on the Home Front). One of the biggest, and most important, of the new ministries was the Ministry of Information, set up on 5 September 1939.

Source A	From a book about Britain after the war, written in 2007.

The first half of the war saw the creation of many new ministries: not only a Ministry of Labour but also Economic Warfare, Food, Home Security, Production, Shipping, Information and Aircraft Production. By 1943, there were well over 250,000 more civil servants [people working for the government] than before the war. It was soon clear that these ministries, as well as the established ones, had to work by centralised, co-ordinated, planning. This produced an utterly different way of looking at government from the old approach.

Source B	A poster issued by the Railway Executive Committee that took control of the railways during the war.

IS YOUR JOURNEY REALLY NECESSARY?

TICKETS

RAILWAY EXECUTIVE COMMITTEE

Activity

Study Source B. Write a sentence on each point to explain:
- why the government took over the railways
- why the person asking the question on the poster is a soldier
- the purpose of the poster.

The Ministry of Information

Learning objectives

In this chapter you will learn about:

- the use of censorship and propaganda
- evaluating the utility or reliability of sources.

Censorship

The most important Ministry of Information (MOI) work was **propaganda** and **censorship**. Censorship is stopping the passing of certain information – in newspapers, radio broadcasts, private letters and even conversations. The aim was to stop information getting out that would encourage the enemy and demoralise the British people. Censors told newspapers and magazines what information and pictures they could (or could not) print. They censored letters going abroad and coming into the country to make sure that important information was not given away. The armed services had their own censors to go through the troops' mail.

Propaganda

Propaganda is giving people information in order to make them think or behave in a particular way. The MOI had been impressed by the Nazis' use of propaganda in the 1930s. It quickly built up a large team of workers to produce posters and leaflets to persuade people to do (and not to do) certain things to help the war effort. It also made 'how to...' films showing people, for example, how to move around safely in the blackout or how to dig a vegetable plot. There were also patriotic short films and newsreels about the war, such as *Britain can take it*. These were shown at the cinema, and MOI vans toured the country showing these films in town and village halls. There were also talks on the radio. The censors made sure that feature films made during the war, such as *The Lion has Wings* and *Henry V*, encouraged patriotic feeling.

Source A From a newspaper article on the autobiography of Ruth Ive, who was a telephone censor in the war. The telephone cables across the Atlantic had been closed down, but there was one 'hot line' in use.

Before a caller was connected, even the King, Ruth had to read aloud this warning: 'The enemy is recording your conversation and will compare it with previous information in his possession. Great discretion is necessary. Any indiscretion will be reported by the Censor to the highest authority.' Once she had to pull the plug on Churchill. He had booked a call to Anthony Eden, who was visiting Canada after a V2 rocket attack in Smithfield [Source E, page 41], with dozens of casualties.

After greeting Eden, Churchill began, 'This morning at 12:00…'. Ive made a split-second judgment, reached for the off switch and warned: 'I must remind you, sir, that there should be no mention of any damage suffered from enemy aircraft. Would you like your call reconnected?' She did this, but Churchill began again, 'Anthony, this morning…'. Ive recalls: 'He sounded so upset, but I had no option but to disconnect him again and warn him of the dangers.'

Source B The censor's office, Liverpool in November 1939, a month after war was declared. At this time, there were 1300 censors working on letters and telegrams.

Source C *From a government leaflet on how to 'make do and mend', published during the war.*

There are a wealth of ideas for letting out children's clothes [undoing the stitches and making the seams smaller to make the garment bigger] An outgrown dress should be completely unpicked from hem to underarms and then along the sleeve seams, so it can be opened flat in one piece. Contrasting bands of material can then be let in at the sides, waist, across the shoulders and along the sleeves if needed.

Source D *Poster produced by the Ministry of Information in 1940.*

"Of course there's no harm in your knowing!"

CARELESS TALK COSTS LIVES

Source E *Poster produced by the Ministry of Information in 1940.*

Activities

1 Study Source D. Hitler never came to Britain so was never under a restaurant table taking notes on what people said. This makes the information in the picture unreliable. Does this mean the source is not useful to a historian? Write a short paragraph to explain your answer.

2 Copy and complete the table below.

Source	A	B	C	D	E
Most useful for…	the extent of censorship				
because…	even Winston Churchill was censored!				

3 How do Sources D and E show how important propaganda was during the war?

Rationing

> ### Learning objectives
>
> In this chapter you will learn about:
> * the impact of the war on the food supply and how the government dealt with it
> * making inferences from sources.

Before the war, Britain **imported** 55 million tons of food a year – 70% of all the food people bought. The Ministry of Food began planning to control the food supply in November 1936, fearing the Germans would sink ships supplying Britain. They were right. By January 1940, German submarines had sunk over 100 ships carrying food to Britain.

Rationing began on 8 January 1940. What was 'on the ration' and the rationed amount changed during the war. People had ration books of coupons. They registered with a shop and the shopkeeper recorded the coupons used. There were three kinds of rationing:

* rationing of foods such as butter by weight
* rationing of dried goods (e.g. flour, biscuits, cereal) and tinned goods on a point system (goods were worth a varying number of points; there was a weekly point maximum)
* government control of foods such as orange juice or milk, where babies, pregnant women or the sick were given supplies first.

The Ministry of Food encouraged people to grow their own food and keep chickens and rabbits. Local parks were turned into allotments to grow crops on. Even the moat around the Tower of London was dug and planted. Many people joined 'pig clubs': buying a pig, sharing its care then sharing the meat when it was killed. But even so, food was scarce and there was little variety. Ministry of Food broadcasts gave recipes and tips for making food go further. People swapped food with their neighbours and shopkeepers favoured regular customers. A 'black market' grew up where you could buy rationed or scarce goods at high prices. The government punished black marketeers and their customers, but it still flourished, especially in cities where people were less able to grow their own food.

Source A	*The average ration for a person for a week in 1941.*

2 oz (56 g) butter
4 oz (113 g) cooking fat
1 oz (28 g) cheese
2 oz (56 g) tea OR coffee
2 oz (56 g) jam or other preserve
4 oz (113 g) bacon or ham
8 oz (226 g) sugar
1 shilling-worth of meat. This bought about 12 oz (340 g) of stewing beef, more of mince, less of steak
1 egg
2 pints (1.1 litres) milk

Source B	*The 'official' recipe for Woolton Pie, from* The Times, *26 April 1941.*

In hotels, restaurants and communal canteens, people have tasted Lord Woolton Pie and found it good. Like many economical dishes, it is good for you and provides necessary vitamins. The ingredients can be varied according to the vegetables in season. Here is the official recipe:
Take 1 lb (500 g) each of potatoes, cauliflower, swede and carrots, 3 or 4 spring onions (if available) 1 teaspoon of vegetable extract and 1 tablespoon of oatmeal. Cook for 10 minutes with just enough water to cover. Stir occasionally, to prevent sticking. Allow to cool. Put into a pie dish, sprinkle with fresh parsley (if available) and cover with a lid of mashed potato or wholemeal pastry. Bake in a hot oven until topping is nicely browned and serve hot with brown gravy.

Source: The Times, *26 April 1941, © The Times/NI Syndication Ltd. 1941*

| Source C | Extracts from the diaries of Clara Milburn, who lived near Coventry during the war. |

8 July 1940: Lord Woolton spoke on the radio. Without warning tea, margarine and cooking fats are to be rationed.

31 December 1940: Lord Woolton asked us to 'go carefully with the tin opener'. Potatoes and oatmeal are plentiful, but we must eat less. He does not want to ration cheese, but asks us to leave it for vegetarians and workers.

7 January 1941: Lord Woolton says the 1s 6d meat ration may have to go down to 1s 3d.

13 February 1941: conversation in Malin's [*the greengrocers*]: 'Any oranges?' 'What a thing to ask, madam, considering the sign on the door!' Mr Malin (interrupting) 'Finch, get Mrs Milburn half a dozen.' The sign said 'No Oranges'.

5 December 1941: Got 5 lbs of apples at the greengrocer. Mrs Malin treats me very kindly – she let me have 3 lbs of potatoes the other day; for regular customers only.

21 September 1942: Saw Mrs Greenslade in town and swapped some pear and apples for a chicken.

| Source D | A Ministry of Food wartime poster. |

BETTER POT-LUCK with Churchill today

THAN HUMBLE PIE

under Hitler tomorrow

DON'T WASTE FOOD!

Activities

1   Work in pairs.

   a   List the things you can learn about rationing from the sources.

   b   Underline things said by more than one source.

2   Read Source B.

   a   Write a description of what you expect Woolton Pie would be like to eat.

   b   List the benefits of the pie, from Lord Woolton's point of view.

ResultsPlus
Build Better Answers

Exam question: What can you learn from Source D about food during the war? (6 marks)

When you are asked what you can learn from a source or sources, you are expected to make *inferences*. This means you work something out from the information in the source; you don't just copy it.

■   **A basic answer (level 1)** just copies the information (for example, *It tells me they told you not to waste food.*)

●   **A good answer (level 2)** makes unsupported inferences from the sources (for example, *they must have been short of food*).

▲   **A better answer (level 3)** makes supported inferences (for example, *the government was saying it was important not to waste food, so important that wasting it could mean Hitler won the war. This probably means it was in short supply.*

Working women

Learning objectives

In this chapter you will learn about:
- the war work women did
- cross-referencing sources.

As with the First World War, the Second World War took huge numbers of men into the armed services. At first, large numbers of unemployed men took over their jobs. But the government re-formed the Women's Land Army in July 1939. It knew that they would need to clear and farm more land to produce the huge amounts of food the country would need when war began. They were right. By March 1940, over 30,000 men had left farming for the army and over 15,000 had left to do other war work. It quickly became clear that women were needed for all types of war work.

Conscription

On 8 December 1941, the government introduced **conscription** for all unmarried women aged 20–30. As the war went on, older single women and then married women were also conscripted. Women could choose to join the armed services, civil defence or industry. They joined all of these in large numbers and were soon doing vital work – by 1943 there were over 100,000 women working on the railways, doing every kind of job from selling tickets to driving the trains.

In the services

Women had their own sections in the armed services: the ATS (army), the WAAF (air force) and the Wrens (navy). At first, their work was almost entirely cleaning, cooking or office work – the war created huge amounts of paperwork. They were also trained as drivers. Women could not go into battle but, as the war progressed, they worked on anti-aircraft posts, as radio operators, as motorbike messengers and even as spies.

Source A — From the autobiography of Joyce Storey, written in 1992, when she was 75 years old.

I went to work at a big engineering firm with huge wartime contracts. The dust, grime and grit with a strong smell of oil and all the machinery awed and scared me, as did the all-male feel of the place. Because of the shortage of men, women were going into foundries and factories. I was put in charge of a huge milling machine. I had to keep the saw covered in lubricating fluid, or it would buckle and a new saw was expensive. Anyway, the Inspector (a man) decided I was good enough to have charge of two of these machines and I was very proud.

Source B — Women bus drivers in Bournemouth learning how to maintain an engine on 14 November 1941.

Source C | *From* Instructions for American Servicemen in Britain, *a booklet issued by the US War Office for soldiers going to fight in Britain in 1942.*

British women officers have stuck to their posts near burning ammunition dumps. They have delivered messages on foot after being blown off their motorcycles. They've pulled airmen from burning planes. They've died at gun posts and, as they fell, another girl has stepped up and carried on. They've won the right to the utmost respect. When you see a girl in uniform with a ribbon on the tunic, remember she didn't get it for knitting more socks than anyone else in Ipswich.

Source D | *From a book written about the Special Operations Executive (SOE) in 1999. The author is writing about F section, which sent 470 people to France altogether.*

The SOE was unusual in that it treated women on a perfect equality with men. For their purposes, there were several jobs that women performed better than men. The French [F] Section sent 39 women to France on missions with the French Resistance, 13 died there. The usual SOE groups consisted of an organiser – usually a man; a courier to take messages – usually a woman; a wireless operator – a man or a woman and a sabotage instructor – always a man.

Source E | *Women maintaining a spitfire plane for the RAF, photographed in 1942.*

Activities

1 Write a sentence explaining how Source D contradicts itself about the position of women in the SOE.

2 Write a note from Joyce Storey (Source A) explaining to a friend how work like hers was vital to the war.

3 Read Source C. Write a circular for British women officers explaining the problems they might have with US servicemen.

4 How far do Sources A, B, C, D and E agree that women were treated equally at work in wartime?

Examination question

What was the purpose of Source C? (8 marks)

Working after the war

Learning objectives

In this chapter you will learn about:
- how women's war work affected post-war employment
- evaluating a hypothesis.

When the war came to an end there was a sudden change to work and the workforce. Millions of men and women were discharged from the services and needed to find civilian jobs. Women who had been 'minding' jobs for servicemen had to give them up when these men came home. Women had to leave the services and war work, too. While attitudes to women working, especially married women, did change because of the war, it was seen as most important to find men work.

Source A *An aircraft factory photographed in January 1930.*

Source B *Statistics of women as part of the workforce for 1931 and 1951, from the Census (all figures in thousands).*

	1931	1951	increase
Women in the workforce	6265	6561	5%
Total workforce (men and women)	21,054	22,210	5%
All women of working age	18,321	20,045	9%
Women as a percentage of the workforce	30%	30%	
Women in the workforce as a percentage of all women of working age	34%	33%	

Source C *Barbara Davies worked at an aircraft factory in Coventry during the war. After the war, she and all the other women in the factory were told they had to leave.*

I went on the night shift one night and was told I was no longer needed. As you can imagine, I wasn't pleased. We went straight round to the **trade union** representative. He said that the jobs were for the men coming out of the forces; that we had to leave the jobs for them. There was nothing we could do at all.

Source D *From a history of Britain written in 1987.*

In 1911, women made up 30% of all non-manual workers. Of nurses and teachers, 63% were women. By 1951, there were two other types of employment in which women were in the majority – clerks (60%) and shop workers (52%). The public were often felt to prefer women to men in these jobs. They were also the jobs in which casual work and low pay were common and women were not seen as posing a threat to the career prospects of men.

Source E *An aircraft factory photographed in March 1951.*

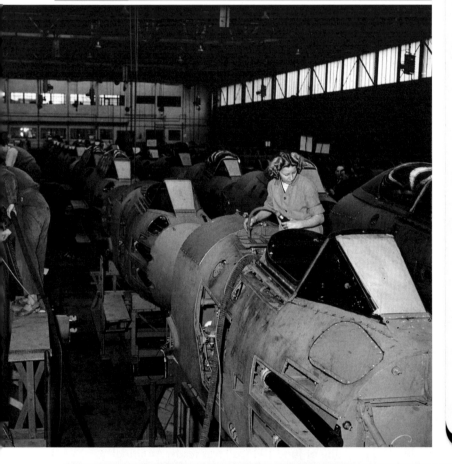

ResultsPlus
Build Better Answers

Exam question: 'After the war, women were expected just to be housewives again.' How far do the sources support this statement?
(16 marks)

In Question 5, when asked how far sources support a statement, it is important to produce a balanced judgment about how far the sources support the statement, using detail from the sources. In this question, you will also get marks for clear presentation and good grammar and spelling.

■ **A basic answer (level 1)** says yes **or** no without specific reference to the sources (for example, *they were seen as only any use in wartime*).

● **A good answer (level 2)** makes a judgment about the statement, referring to the sources, but not in detail and not at length (for example, *Source E shows women working in 1951. They haven't gone back to being housewives*).

▲ **A better answer (level 3)** develops a level 2 answer, usually deciding on either support or the lack of it (for example, *Source E shows women working in 1951. They haven't gone back to being housewives. Source B supports the idea too – there is not a huge drop of numbers of women in the workforce*).

▲ **An excellent answer (level 4)** considers the extent of support, showing both support and the lack of it, with clear examples from the sources. It then delivers a balanced answer, taking into account the reliability of the sources.

Activities

1 Write a short newspaper report headed: Working women 1931–1951: change or continuity? Use the statistics in Source B.

2 In groups, prepare to debate the statement below, using the sources as evidence.
Women had greater job opportunities after the Second World War than before it.

D-Day

> ### Learning objectives
>
> In this chapter you will learn about:
> - what led up to D-Day and how it was planned
> - making inferences from sources.

On 7 December 1941, the Japanese, who were **allies** of Germany, bombed the US naval base at Pearl Harbor, Hawaii. The USA, which had been sending money and supplies to Britain, finally decided to enter the war against Germany and Japan. However, in US eyes, the main war was in the Pacific, against Japan. They did not want to fight in both Europe and the Pacific for long, so suggested a plan for a quick invasion of Europe.

Operation Overlord

The British convinced US generals that an invasion had to be carefully planned. Germany had had years to plan defences along the French coast. Even though they were diverting troops to fight the Soviets in the east, there were still huge numbers in France. The Allies could only land as many troops at a time as they had landing craft. They needed careful planning to land as many as possible, as quickly as possible. They also needed to plan to send more troops and supplies quickly. They needed to divert as many German troops as possible from Normandy, the planned landing site. So they carefully leaked information suggesting they were planning to invade a different part of the coast.

The date chosen for the invasion was changed several times. It was dependent on the weather, the build-up of troops and equipment in the south of England and reaching a point where enough of the *Luftwaffe* had been destroyed to stop it posing a huge threat to the invaders. The invasion was finally set for the night of 6 June 1944.

Source A — *From a modern dictionary of the Second World War, published in 1995.*

Early in 1942, a report by Lt General Eisenhower drew attention to the problem facing the United States in fighting a war in two different places with limited resources. A plan to build up US forces in Britain was presented to President Roosevelt, codename Bolero, which planned an invasion of Europe within a year. Churchill was furiously opposed to the plan, which he and the British military chiefs considered impetuous folly.

It became clear the invasion of Europe could not be mounted before 1944. A combined Anglo-American headquarters was set up in England in April 1943, to co-ordinate planning and, most importantly, to supervise the hugely complex and widespread deception plans being carried out by the Allies and resistance agents all over Europe.

Source B — *From a modern history of the Second World War, published in 1989.*

In August 1942, there was a reconnaissance raid on the French coastal town of Dieppe, to see what the problems of capturing a French port were. The problems were enormous: over 3000 men and a destroyer were lost. It was clear that no attacks could be made on the French coast without enough support from the air and sea.

By the beginning of June 1944, all was ready. An initial force of over 100,000 men was waiting to be sent from 4000 landing craft, supported by over 250 warships and 11,000 aircraft. To help land men and equipment scientists had designed two floating harbours, called Mulberries, to be towed across the Channel. An enormous pipeline to carry over a million tons of fuel every day under the Channel, known as Pluto, was also to be laid. To confuse the Germans, fake bombing raids were made in Norway and Calais.

Allied gains at D-Day and in the weeks that followed. Utah, Omaha, Gold, Juno and Sword were the five main landing sites of the Allied invasion.

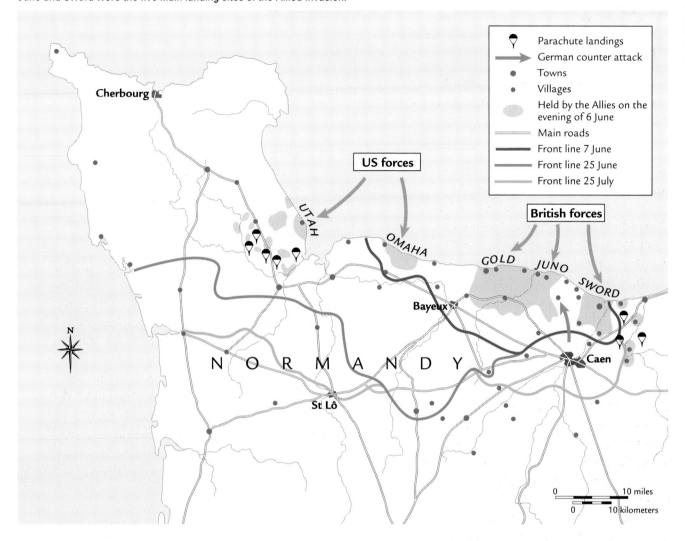

Source C — *From a modern history of the Second World War, published in 1970.*

Before its launch, the invasion of Normandy looked a most hazardous plan. Yet the first footholds were soon expanded into a large bridgehead 80 miles wide [an area of Allied-held land]. The enemy never managed to stop the Allies moving outwards and the whole German position in France quickly collapsed. But at the start, the line between success and failure was narrow. The ultimate triumph has obscured the fact that the Allies were in great danger at the outset and had a very close shave.

Activities

1 In groups, discuss what you can learn from Sources B and C about the planning involved in Operation Overlord. Compile a group list.

2 Telegrams were usually very short, not in sentences, using as few words as possible to make a point (for example, 'Home 3 pm meet train'). Write a telegram from a British general to a US general, summing up why invading Europe without careful planning was a bad idea.

3 The written sources in this chapter all come from books written after the time using many different histories and memoirs. Write a sentence or two to explain what makes such sources useful here.

Why did D-Day succeed?

Learning objectives

In this chapter you will learn about:
● the reasons for D-Day's success
● evaluating a hypothesis.

D-Day was a success, thanks to careful planning and preparation. It was impossible to stop the Germans seeing troops, planes and ships gathering on the coast to invade. But they were confused about where the troops would land by:

● attacks on **radar** stations all along the Channel and up as far as Norway
● coded radio messages and other information leaked by resistance groups and the SOE, all suggesting the invasion would be near Calais
● a variety of complicated plans that led the Germans to believe that large numbers of troops were landing in other parts of France and that a large fleet of ships was moving towards the French coast near Calais.

Other factors

Deception was important, but Overlord needed more than that to work. The Pluto fuel pipeline, the rapid ferrying of troops and supplies once the invasion began and the air and sea backup were all vital to the actual invasion. If you look at the map on page 55 you will see that parachute troops captured inland areas on the first day. They helped the resistance to blow up railway lines and bridges and to disrupt German communications. The US provided huge numbers of troops and a great deal of equipment, so, while losses on the first day were heavy, the Allies could keep going and keep up the pressure. The German army was under pressure in the east and in the Mediterranean (Rome was captured from the Germans on 4 June) and was not able to easily regroup and organise to fight back.

Source A *From a history of the SOE, written in 1998.*

Two three-man teams from the SAS were dropped near the Cherbourg Peninsula to convince the Germans that the Normandy landings were only a diversion, and that the main assault was in the Pas de Calais. They were part of 'Fortitude', a deception scheme to fool the enemy into sending reinforcements to the wrong beach heads. Six SAS couldn't be mistaken for an army of invaders, so hundreds of dummies were dropped with them to give the impression of a major landing. Each team had record players to play the sound of pistol fire and soldiers' voices and had flares to light up the sky. The Germans immediately rushed troops to the area to repel the invaders and resistance workers attacked them as they went to add conviction.

Source B *From the D-Day memories of a German soldier, published on a history website.*

There was a strong wind, thick cloud and enemy planes had not bothered us more than usual. But that night the air was full of countless planes. We thought, 'What are they demolishing tonight?' Then it started. I was at the wireless set. One message followed the other. 'Parachutists landed here, gliders reported there,' and finally 'landing craft approaching.' Some of our guns fired as best they could. In the morning, a huge naval force was seen – the last report our observation posts sent before they were overwhelmed. And it was the last report we had about the situation. It was no longer possible to get any idea of what was happening. Wireless communications were jammed, the cables cut and our officers had lost their grasp of the situation. Troops streaming back told us their position on the coast had been overrun or that the few 'bunkers' in our sector had either been shot up or blown to pieces.

Source C *From A Dictionary of the Second World War, published in 1995.*

Perhaps the single most important factor in the success of Overlord was the deceptions, which relied on Ultra [the British cracking of German signalling codes], which enabled the Allies to monitor the German response to their deceptions and adjust their planning accordingly.

Source D *From a speech by Winston Churchill to the House of Commons on 6 June 1944.*

I can state to the House that this operation is proceeding in a thoroughly satisfactory manner. Many dangers and difficulties, which at this time last night appeared extremely formidable, are behind us. We have crossed the sea with far less loss than we feared. The resistance of the batteries was greatly weakened by the bombing of the Air Force, and the superior bombardment of our ships quickly reduced their fire to a minimum. The landings of the troops on a broad front, both British and American Allied troops along the whole front, have been effective. Our troops have penetrated, in some cases, several miles inland. The outstanding feature has been the landings of airborne troops on a scale far larger than anything previously. These landings took place with extremely little loss and with great accuracy. Particular anxiety attached to them, because problems with the light and the weather. Many things might have happened at the last minute to prevent airborne troops from playing their part. Fighting is in progress at various points. We captured various bridges which were of importance, and which were not blown up. There is even fighting proceeding in the town of Caen.

Results Plus

Top Tip

When asked to consider how far the sources support a statement, good answers consider *the lack of* support as well as support in the sources. The best answers also consider how reliable or typical the sources are.

Source E *US trucks, jeeps and other supplies being ferried to Normandy a few days after the invasion began.*

Activities

1 Turn the paragraph of text headed 'Other factors' on page 56 into a bulleted list of factors for success.

   a Underline the factor supported by Source E.

   b Circle the factor supported by Source D.

2 Write two or three sentences explaining how far Sources A, B, C, D and E support the following statement:

   The most important factor behind D-Day's success was the way the Germans were misled.

The defeat of Germany

Learning objectives

In this chapter you will learn about:
- the reasons for Germany's defeat
- cross-referencing sources.

Following D-Day, Germany was under pressure from all sides (see Source A). It had been straining its resources to produce the supplies it needed for many months. It was also running out of soldiers. The Allies put pressure on Germany by:

- bombing industrial sites, military bases and cities in Germany, far more heavily that Britain had been bombed in the **Blitz**

- using radar to find enemy submarines and bombing them from planes, so keeping the seas clear to ship supplies

- helping resistance movements to fight the Germans and sabotage road and rail links.

The Allies did not have a smooth path to victory. British and US commanders made military errors. The Allied armies suffered high losses at Arnhem in September 1944, where they tried to liberate the Netherlands, take control of the road networks and cross the Rhine into Germany. Unlike the D-Day planning, the plans for this were hurried and only 2827 of the 10,300 troops involved survived.

Some German leaders planned an assassination of Hitler, but it failed. Hitler got rid of everyone who might have been a conspirator and pushed his armies on in the east and at the Rhine. Following the German victory at Arnhem, in December 1944, the Germans launched a surprise counter attack westwards – the Battle of the Bulge – but the Germans lost men they could not replace, while the Allies brought in reinforcements. By April, Soviet troops were closing in on Berlin. Hitler committed suicide and Germany surrendered.

Source A *Allied advances 1942–5.*

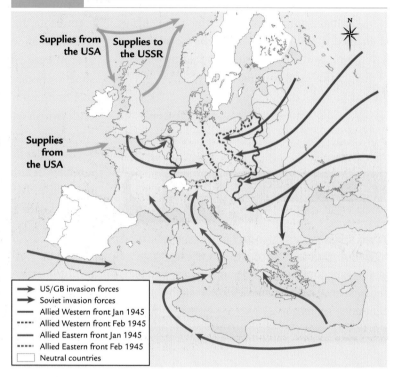

- → US/GB invasion forces
- → Soviet invasion forces
- — Allied Western front Jan 1945
- ----- Allied Western front Feb 1945
- — Allied Eastern front Jan 1945
- ----- Allied Eastern front Feb 1945
- ▢ Neutral countries

Source B *From a textbook on the world since 1914, published in 1989.*

It was the massive production of the USA that made victory certain in the end. Factories in Britain and the USSR worked long and hard and produced more than seemed possible. But many of their factories had suffered war damage and they were short of raw materials and workers. In the USA there was plenty of everything and no war damage. Out of the factories poured a stream of tanks, guns, ships, trucks, planes – everything needed for war. They went not just to the US forces but to the other Allies as well.

ResultsPlus
Watch out!

The various ways of referring to Russia under communist rule can be confusing. It is sometimes called the USSR (Union of Socialist Soviet Republics) and sometimes the Soviet Union. Other people refer to it as Russia.

| Source C | A cartoon published in a British newspaper on 19 January 1945. Panzers were German tanks. It is referring to a wartime joke: 'If we only had some ham, we could make ham and eggs.' 'If we only had the eggs.' |

ELASTIC DEFENCE

| Source D | Production of weaponry 1939–45 (the USA did not start production until it entered the war in December 1941). |

Country	Tanks	Aircraft	Rifles	Allied military ships or German submarines
Germany	6300	89,500	10,328,000	954
USA	99,500	192,000	12,330,000	8812
USSR	102,000	112,100	12,139,000	161
UK	29,300	94,600	2,457,000	1156

ResultsPlus
Build Better Answers

Exam question: Do Sources B, C and D support the view that resources were the deciding factor in Germany's defeat? Explain your answer. (10 marks)

■ **A basic answer (level 1)** does not refer to evidence from the sources.

● **A good answer (level 2)** says yes and/or no with support from the sources (for example, *Yes, Sources B and D agree that the USA had lots more resources and so could go on supplying Allied troops*).

▲ **A better answer (level 3)** considers the amount of support given (for example, *They are all about resources. Source B says the USA had huge resources and Source D shows how much. Source C is implying that Germany's resources are running out. But Source C also suggests that disrupted communications was a part of defeat too – the Germans were running out of resources **and** couldn't move it around easily even if they had it. Source C is only a cartoon, so it's telling us the cartoonist's view, not the actual situation*)

▲ **An excellent answer (top of level 3)** considers all of the above and also considers how reliable the source is.

Activities

1 Write two or three sentences to explain whether Sources A and B support the idea that the Germans lost because the Allies had more resources.

2 Design a poster using the information in Source B: 'We won the war because…'.

60

In the Unit 3 examination, you will be required to answer five questions. You have only one hour and 15 minutes to answer these questions, so the examiners are not expecting you to write huge amounts. The number of marks given in the answer book help you judge how much to write. The time allocation to the right gives a little thinking time before you put pen to paper and a few minutes to read through your answers at the end.

Question 1:	10 minutes
Question 2:	12 minutes
Question 3:	12 minutes
Question 4:	12 minutes
Question 5:	20 minutes

Here, we are going to look at Question 4. The question below is based on the chapter in Key Topic 3 called 'The Ministry of Information' (on pages 46–47).

Results Plus
Maximise your marks

Question 4

Examiner's tip: Question 4 will ask you to consider the utility (usefulness) and reliability (accuracy) of two sources. Remember:

- usefulness is about what you can find out from a source
- reliability is whether you can believe it.

'How useful are Sources A and D on pages 46–47 as evidence of the restrictions imposed by the government in the Second World War? Explain your answer. (10 marks)

Student answer

I think both of these sources are very useful because they are from the time and because they tell you useful information. Source A tells you that they had people who censored phone calls, even the prime minister's. Source D tells you they used posters to get their message across that careless talk costs lives.

Examiner comment

This is a very basic answer. The first sentence is no more than level 1 as it is undeveloped and does not give any support from the sources. The answer then moves on to the information that can be found in the sources. Although detail is given, there is no interpretation, nor any consideration of the nature, origin or purpose of the sources. So the mark would be a low level 2 at best.

Let's rewrite the answer with some more thought given to the information in the sources.

I think both of these sources are very useful because they are from the time and because they tell you useful information. Source A tells you that they had people who censored phone calls, even the prime minister's, and that most people couldn't make phone calls anyway, so the government was really stopping people talking. Source D tells you they used posters to get their message across that careless talk costs lives, which is again stopping people from talking. So the sources tell us that the government is concerned that people will give away information. They really want restrict the amount of information that people give to other people.

This is a better answer in that the candidate is now 'looking behind' the information provided to show how the sources can be used as evidence of government policy, rather than just concentrating on what they say. There is enough here to get you over half marks (so it is a level 2 answer), but you will need to do more to reach level 3. There is still no attempt to consider how the nature, origin or purpose of the source affects the reliability of the sources – and therefore, their utility.

Let's rewrite the answer, adding the analysis.

They are useful in telling you the level of government control over what you could say. Source A tells you that they had people who censored phone calls, even the prime minister's, and that most people couldn't make phone calls anyway, so the government was really stopping people talking. Source D tells you they used posters to get their message across that careless talk costs lives, which is again stopping people from talking.
So it shows that the government believes that people giving away information in public is dangerous and they want to try to restrict this by putting up posters to remind people not to do it and also by controlling the way people communicate. Mind you, the story in Source A is one of those stories that people could well add to to make themselves seem more important. And while you know that the use of phones was restricted, you have no idea how often a phone censor didn't stop people. However, Source A is very useful in showing how much they wanted to stop people talking – it is very shocking. But both these sources only tell you about communication restrictions. You have no idea how they restricted travel, for instance, or food buying.

Now we have a top-level answer (level 3). It shows some good interpretation and a consideration of how the origin of one of the sources affects its reliability and, therefore, how much we can make of it.

Key Topic 4: Labour in power 1945–51

Once the Second World War had ended, the British government faced many difficult tasks. In Europe, British politicians and the British army had to take part in the political settlement, while British aid organisations helped the millions of refugees who had been displaced by the war. Back in Britain, there were many problems caused by the war, which the government also had to deal with. These included a huge war debt to the USA, which made the government reluctant to commit to spending on welfare.

In this Key Topic, you will study:

- Labour comes to power
- responding to Beveridge: the attack on 'want'
- the NHS.

You will see how the newly elected Labour government worked to identify the most pressing social problems in post-war Britain and how they then set out to solve them. You will consider the many difficulties they faced in doing this, including opposition to their plans from those who were asked to put them into practice – for example the opposition of many doctors to the idea of a National Health Service.

Labour comes to power

Learning objectives

In this chapter you will learn about:
- why Labour won the 1945 election
- making inferences from sources.

Although the war with Japan was still going on, the end of the war in Europe in May 1945 seemed like the end of the whole war to many people. Hitler had been their enemy and Hitler was beaten. Britain's towns and cities were safe from bombing.

So, even though many people were away fighting in the Pacific or were in Europe dealing with the aftermath of Germany's defeat, people in Britain were thinking about the future. Bombing had made many people homeless. **Rationing** was worse, not better. Once the war was over, farmers needed time to grow crops again. Factories needed time to switch from war production to making clothes and other goods again, so there were still shortages. People wanted homes, jobs and a chance for a better life. But what kind of government would provide this?

Calling an election

When the war ended, the coalition government had to decide what to do next. Churchill (the Conservative leader and prime minister) and Clement Attlee (Labour leader and Churchill's deputy when he was abroad) wanted to keep the coalition going until Japan was beaten. The Labour Party and the Liberals rejected this idea. They wanted a fresh start for the country.

In some ways, it suited Churchill to have an election close to the end of the war in Europe, as he could benefit from the popularity of his war leadership. On 23 May 1945, he resigned and an election date was set for 5 July.

Source A From the Conservative Party **manifesto** for the 1945 election. Instead of saying 'we believe', as was usual in something written for a party, this one said 'I' – meaning Churchill.

I had hoped the Coalition Government would continue until the end of the war with Japan. The Labour and Liberal Parties were unwilling to agree, so a general election is inevitable. I have formed a new National Government, of the best men in all parties. It is a strong government, and contains many who helped me run the country through the darkest days and on whose advice and ability I rely.

We seek the good of the whole nation. We believe the unity of the British people is greater than class or party differences. This unity enabled us to stand like a rock against Germany when she overran Europe.

Source B Winston Churchill campaigning in London in 1945.

The election campaign

The Conservative campaign focused on Churchill, not the party – one slogan was 'Let Him Finish The Job'. They promised new homes and support for the poor and unemployed. But many Conservative politicians had previously opposed such reforms in parliament. They misjudged how much the nation wanted these reforms and were too confident in Churchill's 'magic'.

Churchill made the first election broadcast; and a big mistake. Maybe he was too used to making speeches against the Nazis. In warning of the dangers of Labour's socialist policies, he said a socialist state would never work without a Gestapo to run it. The Gestapo were the Nazi secret police. He was comparing the Labour Party to the Nazis, despite the fact that Clement Atlee, a Labour politician, had been his deputy for much of the war. The campaign never really recovered. The election was on 5 July and the results did not come out until 26 July, to allow for postal votes from those in the forces abroad. Labour won.

Examination question

What can you learn from Source A about what people wanted from a post-war government?

(6 marks)

Source C *From a letter written by Dennis Healey, who became a Labour MP, to a friend in February 1945.*

I am only one of hundreds of young men, now in the forces, who long to fight an election for the Labour Party. We represent millions of soldiers, sailors and airmen who want socialism and have been fighting to save a world where socialism is possible – it is a matter of life and death for them…We have almost won the war, at the highest price ever paid for victory. If you could see the shattered misery that was once Italy: the wrecked villages; Cassino, with a bomb-created river washing green slime through rubble that once was homes; you would see that the defeat of Hitler and Mussolini is not enough to justify the destruction of twenty centuries of Europe. Only a more glorious future can make up for this wiping out of the past.

Source D *A Labour Party poster for the 1945 election. Why does it stress the peace?*

AND NOW– WIN THE <u>PEACE</u>

VOTE LABOUR

Published by the LABOUR PARTY, Transport House, Smith Square, London, S.W.; and Printed by Maycroft Press, Ltd. London.

Source E *From the Labour party manifesto for the 1945 election.*

They say, 'Full employment. Yes! If we can get it without interfering too much with private industry.' We say, 'Full employment in any case, and if we need to keep a firm public hand on industry in order to get jobs for all, very well. No more dole queues, in order to let the Czars of Big Business remain kings in their own castles. The price of so-called 'economic freedom' for the few is too high if it is bought at the cost of idleness and misery for millions.'

Source F *Part of Churchill's radio speech, 4 June 1945.*

I must tell you that a socialist policy is opposed to British ideas on freedom. There is to be one State, which all must obey. This State, once in power, will tell everyone what to do: where to work, what to work at, where they may go and what they may say, what they may think, where their wives are to queue up for the State ration, and what education their children are to receive. A socialist state could not afford opposition. No socialist system can work without a political police. They would have to fall back on some form of Gestapo.

Source G *Part of Clement Atlee's ironical radio reply to Source F.*

I can only suppose Mr Churchill wanted the electors to understand how great the difference is between Mr Churchill, the Great Leader in war of a united nation and Mr Churchill the Conservative party leader. He feared that those who had accepted his leadership in war might be tempted, out of gratitude, to follow him further. I thank him for having disillusioned them so thoroughly.

Source H *Election results, 1945.*

Party	Number of votes	Seats in parliament
Labour	11,967,746	393
Conservative	9,101,099	197
Liberal	2,252,430	12
Others (five parties)	1,168,538	21

Activities

1 Read Source A.

   a Write a sentence to explain how Churchill suggests a Conservative vote is a vote for the war government.

   b Write a sentence explaining why he might think this was a good thing.

   c Write a slogan for his election campaign, based on this part of the manifesto.

2 The cartoonist who drew Source I wanted people to realise how foolish Churchill was to suggest the Labour Party could be like the Nazi Party. List all the elements in the cartoon that make you think this.

3 Write a short paragraph for each of Sources C and I, explaining what the source tells you about why Labour came to power.

Source I *A cartoon from a British newspaper published on 7 June 1945, three days after Churchill's 'Gestapo' speech (Source F).*

LIFE UNDER THE ATTLEE TERROR !!

VICTIM TORTURED FOR MAKING A NAUGHTY SPEECH !!!

DREAMLAND

The Beveridge Report

> ## Learning objectives
>
> In this chapter you will learn about:
> - the Beveridge Report and its importance
> - considering the purpose of a source.

During the war, Ernest Bevin, the **minister** of labour (and a member of the Labour Party) set up a committee to suggest how to improve life in Britain after the war. William Beveridge, who had worked on several committees studying social problems, was its chairman.

On 1 December 1942, the Beveridge report, over 300 pages long, was published. Many MPs (most of them Conservative) disagreed strongly with its recommendations, but realised it had a huge amount of public support. It sold over 70,000 copies in the first few days.

The recommendations

The report said the state should support its citizens 'from the cradle to the grave' – from birth until death. It had to fight 'five giants':

- **want:** the lack of basic needs such as food
- **ignorance:** the lack of proper education for all
- **disease:** the lack of proper medical care for all
- **squalor:** poor living conditions
- **idleness:** unemployment.

As the government took control of more and more aspects of life during the war, it changed people's views on how government worked and what parts of life it was responsible for. Even Conservative MPs saw it would be harder to avoid welfare responsibilities once the war was over.

ResultsPlus
Watch out!

Don't be confused by the use of the word 'idleness' in the report and elsewhere. It did not mean laziness – although it was sometimes also used in that way, especially by people who wanted to criticise the unemployed. It meant being out of work.

Source A   *Part of a radio broadcast made by William Beveridge on 2 December 1942, the day after the Beveridge Report was published. Think about who would have been listening to the broadcast.*

My report is a plan for social security. It will make sure that no one in Britain, willing to work if he can, is without enough money to meet the essential needs of himself and his family.

The scheme has three parts. Firstly, an all-in social insurance scheme of cash **benefits**. Secondly, a scheme of children's allowances, for all children. Thirdly, an all-in scheme of medical assistance at all times for everybody.

Source B   *The official notes of a Cabinet meeting on 15 February 1943. These notes were not made public until 2006.*

On 15 February, the **Cabinet** discussed what to say in the debate on whether to introduce legislation to give effect to the Beveridge Plan during that Parliament. It was pointed out that if they were to be ready to deal with post-war problems they needed to start planning.

The Cabinet agreed the Government should not be committed to introducing legislation for the reform of social services during the war but should not put themselves in a position where it was impossible to introduce such legislation.

Prime minister stated: Impossible to predict the international situation after war. Make no promises; give no commitments; but make every possible preparation.

The Beveridge Report

Source C · *Part of a speech by Labour MP James Griffiths during the parliamentary debate on the Beveridge Report.*

I have given the people of the town I represent a promise I must not break. I have said, 'You are asked to leave your homes, your work and your community – for the sake of the country. When the war is over I will do my best to see you are given decent jobs or, if they are not available, that you will have an income that will keep your family from want.'

Source E *Part of a speech made by Winston Churchill at the Lord Mayor's Lunch in London on 9 November 1943. Think about who would have been listening to the speech.*

I regard it as a definite part of the responsibility of this National Government to have plans perfected to make sure that in the years immediately after the war, food, work and homes are found for all. The war would not be won unless there was a policy of food, work and homes after victory for the men and women who fought and won.

Source D A cartoon published on 17 February 1943, over two months after the Beveridge Report was published.

Examination question

What can you learn from Source D about reactions to the Beveridge Report? (6 marks)

Activities

1 Write a sentence to explain:
   - the message of Source A
   - the purpose of Source A.

2 Do the same for Sources C and D.

3 Write a sentence explaining what Source D suggests about Churchill's feeling about the Beveridge Report.

4 Does Source B support this (remember Churchill was prime minister)?

Fighting giants

Learning objectives

In this chapter you will learn about:
- the attack on the five giants, especially 'want'
- considering the purpose of a source.

People in Britain approved of the Beveridge Report. They wanted the government to fight his five giants. From the publication of the report in December 1942 up to the election of 1945, the government debated what changes to make and how and when to make them. The National Government had set up free milk and free school meals in 1942, but as a wartime measure. What permanent measures did it take?

Before the election, apart from debating possible laws, The National Government passed the *Education Act* of 1944 that restructured the school system and provided free education to the age of 15.

It passed the *Family Allowances Act* of 1945, which paid mothers 5 shillings a week for every child after the first one. Payments did not actually begin until August 1946, so the Labour government (by then in power) got the credit for them in the eyes of many people. The Labour government was elected because many people felt sure a Conservative government would not act on Beveridge's recommendations. Certainly it was the Labour government that brought in the other measures that provided wide-ranging state support for everyone (see Source C).

| Source A | This photograph, used in newspapers at the time, shows a mother and her five children at a London post office on 6 August 1946. She is collecting her first week's family allowance payment of £1 (5 shillings for each child except the eldest). Her husband, if he was an ordinary worker, would have been earning about £7 a week. Think how the extra income might have affected their lives. |

Source B *From the* Daily Mail *newspaper for 5 July 1948. A farm worker, among the lowest paid in 1948, earned £4 10s a week.*

On Monday morning you will wake in a new Britain, in a state that takes over its citizens six months before they are born, providing free care and services for their early years, their schooling, sickness, workless days, widowhood, retirement and death. All this with free doctoring, dentistry and medicine – all for 4s 11d of your weekly pay packet.

Source C *Laws to fight the Beveridge Report giants up to 1948.*

☐ Coalition government

☐ Labour government

FIVE GIANTS

Idleness

From 1945 Government building schemes provide work

Want

1945 Family Allowances Act
- 5s a week for each child after the first one

1946 National Insurance Act
- Workers pay 4s 11d into the National Insurance Scheme
- Employers also contribute
- The government provides unemployment, maternity and sickness benefit and old age pensions

1946 National Assistance Act
- Poor Law and earlier benefits abolished
- National Assistance Boards set up to provide government help to homeless, disabled and mentally ill

Ignorance

1944 Education Act
- Free education up to 14

1947 Education Act
- Free education up to 15

Squalor

1946 New Towns Act
- 17 new towns built in England and 4 towns (Crawley, Peterborough, Northampton and Warrington) enlarged hugely
- 5 new towns in Scotland, 1 in Wales
- Huge local authority house-building programme: by September 1948, 750,000 new homes built (the amount destroyed in the war)

Disease

1946 National Health Services (NHS) Act
- Free medical, dental and eye care for all

1947 NHS Act
- Charges on prescriptions

1947 NHS Act
- Charges on some services

Build Better Answers

Exam question: What was the purpose of publishing the photograph (Source A)? Use detail from the photo and your own knowledge to explain the answer. **(8 marks)**

■ **A basic answer (level 1)** makes generalised statements without reference to the source or their knowledge (for example, *People got child benefit*).

● **A good answer (level 2)** considers the **message** of the source and supports it with reference to the source or their own knowledge (for example, *It is saying you can now get child benefit and people will be better off*).

▲ **A better answer (level 3)** also considers the **purpose** of the source (for example, *It is saying you can now get child benefit and people will be better off. It wants people who read the paper to know about child benefit and to support it. The mother looks very happy to be getting the benefit. Also, they have chosen a family that looks happy and clean, not dirty and sullen*).

Activities

1 Write a paragraph explaining what Source B tells you about the Welfare State.

2 Use Source C to write an explanation of how the laws might affect:
- an unemployed builder with four children
- a bank manager in a small town in the south of England with two children.

A National Health Service

Learning objectives

In this chapter you will learn about:
- planning the NHS and opposition from the medical profession
- evaluating the utility or reliability of sources.

Beveridge suggested a free national health service in his 1942 report. But doctors at all levels were suspicious of state control of their profession. The British Medical Association (BMA), to which many doctors belonged, had a long history of disputes with the government.

The BMA and the government

The BMA had objected to the 1911 introduction of free medical care for those paying National Insurance contributions – care by a chosen 'panel' of doctors and only for the contributor, not his family. They fought all changes that increased free healthcare, especially the 1941 law that raised the income of people who could claim from £250 to £420. But by the time war broke out even the BMA admitted that the health service needed reforms. It was a muddle of free panels and private care, while hospitals and clinics were run privately or by **voluntary groups**.

Working together?

The BMA sat on government committees during the war to try to agree on a new health service but reaching agreement was difficult. They disagreed with the government over the level of government control, over who should get free healthcare and how doctors should be paid. When the Labour government came to power in 1945, the new minister of health, Aneurin Bevan, consulted the BMA, but pushed the law through at the same time. The National Health Act, passed in November 1946, was due to come into force in January 1948. Disputes with the BMA delayed it to April then July 1948.

Source A — *From a book about the development of the National Health Service written in 1988.*

The BMA had deep fears of state control. By 1943, its doctors were in confrontation with the government, not only to defend their independence, but also over past disputes. They opposed the official plan on every level. They were particularly against working for local authorities, saying this turned a profession that managed itself into a local government service.

Source B — *Written by Dr Charles Hill of the BMA, in a 1944 book on health and social welfare.*

For years, the BMA has pressed for reorganisation of the structure of the country's medical services. These have grown up, over the last hundred years, piece by piece with no co-ordination. The result is a confused muddle. A comprehensive medical service should be available to all who need it; but it is unnecessary for the state to provide it for those who can provide for themselves. The best medical service will be provided by independent professionals working with the government, rather than by doctors controlled by a bureaucracy.

Source C — *From a book about the National Health Service written in 1952.*

In January 1948, the BMA asked members: Do you approve, or disapprove, of the National Health Services Act, 1946, in its present form? The voting was 40,814 votes against and 4,735 for. On 17 March, the BMA voted not to enter the new service until it was changed. The Minister made changes to the pay and the restriction of private practice. Another vote was held. The BMA advised non-co-operation unless at least 13,000 were for it. This time the vote was 14,620 for the act with changes and 25,842 against. At a BMA meeting on 28 May it was decided to recommend doctors to take part in the service.

Source D *From the* Guardian *newspaper, 6 May 1948.*

The National Health Service is saved. A majority of doctors are still against parts of the act. But the there are so many fewer against than in the February vote that the BMA has decided to advise the doctors to co-operate. It is a brave, as well as a wise, decision. It is important that people do not expect a magic change on July 5 and do not blame doctors if at first things do not work perfectly. We should be grateful that the BMA have been able to overcome their feelings of doubt and do what most people outside the profession see as the right thing.

Examination question

Exam question: 'How useful are sources C and E as evidence of doctors' opposition to the NHS? **(10 marks)**

Source E *A cartoon published in a newspaper on 15 January 1948. The person being chopped up is Bevan, the minister of health.*

OPERATION SABOTAGE

Activities

1 In pairs, discuss the message and purpose of Source E. Write a sentence to explain:
   * what bias the cartoonist has and how you know this
   * whether this bias stops the source being useful to a historian studying the NHS.
2 Write a sentence for each of the following, explaining which source you would use to show it and why:
   * why the BMA objected to the NHS Act
   * why the BMA eventually advised members to join the system.

Using the NHS

Learning objectives

In this chapter you will learn about:
- the impact of the NHS up to 1951
- cross-referencing sources.

The NHS was wildly popular; the government badly underestimated how much it would cost. Glasses and false teeth were the most popular, but the medicine bill was also high. By 1949, the government was debating introducing charges. *The National Health Service Act* of 1949 set a 1-shilling prescription charge (the old, poor or disabled did not have to pay). It did not actually come into force until 1952. Bevan disagreed, and resigned as Minister of Health because of it. Another Act, in 1951, put a charge of 1 shilling towards the cost of glasses or half the cost of false teeth (again, the old, poor or disabled did not have to pay). These charges were fiercely objected to, but even when they were in force, those who needed free treatment were getting it, a vast improvement on the situation before the war.

Source A A cartoon first printed in a newspaper on 24 August 1948. The caption said: 'Absolutely free – but you'd better get cracking before the supplies run out.'

Source B Alice Law remembers going to keep her mother company as she tried out the various services of the NHS in 1948.

Everything was just a few minutes' walk away. She went to the optician's and got new glasses on prescription from the doctor. Then she went further down the road to the chiropodist and had her feet seen to. Then she went back to the doctor, because she'd been having trouble with her ears. He said he'd fix her up with a hearing aid.

Source C From the National Archive website article on the NHS, written in the 1990s.

Demand for health care under the new National Health Service (NHS) exceeded all predictions. The number of patients on doctors' registers rose to 30 million. The NHS budgeted £1 million for opticians, but within a year, 5.25 million prescriptions for glasses and other work had produced a bill of £32 million. In 1947, doctors wrote 7 million prescriptions a month, which rose to 19 million per month in 1951.
The poor gained access to doctors and a range of treatments previously beyond their means, and no longer needed to worry economically about illness or injury. But it was not only the poor who benefited. The middle classes also made full use of the NHS. In the first year, from a total of 240,000 hospital beds, only 2.5% were private. Over 95% of doctors joined the NHS.

| Source D | From an interview with John Marks for an NHS website in 2008. Marks qualified as a doctor in 1948 and went straight to work in the NHS. |

'The evening of the day the NHS started the exam results were announced. I was a doctor.'

Nine days later, John Marks registered with the General Medical Council and went straight into a job in Shoreditch at £250 a year.

'The demand when the NHS started was unbelievable. Before the health service started, there was guaranteed treatment through National Health Insurance for low-paid workers (the panel system), but even then their families were excluded. There was an enormous amount of demand for surgery for previously untreated conditions. Also for things like wigs and, in some places, free cotton wool.'

| Source E | Government spending on the NHS each year from 1948 to 1952 (1948–9 is from July), estimate and actual. |

Year	Estimated cost in £s	Actual cost in £s
1948–49	198,376,000	275,904,542
1949–50	352,324,600	449,171,732
1950–51	464,514,400	465,019,300
1951–52	469,127,700	470,551,200

Results Plus

Top Tip

When discussing how far sources support a statement, students will get the best marks in their level if they cross-refer between sources, as well as checking each source against the statement.

Results Plus

Build Better Answers

Exam question: How far do sources A, B and D support the view that people exploited the NHS when it began? (10 marks)

In Question 3, when asked a question about the support given by selected sources, be sure to cross-refer between sources and consider how typical/reliable supporting sources are.

■ **A basic answer (level 1)** makes a generalised comment (for example, *People used the NHS to get things like false teeth and glasses*).

● **A good answer (level 2)** finds evidence in the sources that shows support and/or the lack of it (for example, *Source A shows a baby with false teeth and glasses, which it does not need, saying these things will run out, which seems to support the statement. But Source B shows an old lady getting what she needs – it doesn't suggest she is misusing the service*).

▲ **A better answer (level 3)** does the same as level 2, but also considers the amount of support given.

▲ **An excellent answer (top of level 3)** also considers how typical or reliable that support is (for example, *Source A shows a baby with false teeth and glasses, which it does not need, saying these things will run out (implying it is misusing the service). But it is a cartoon and cartoons often exaggerate things. Source B has an old lady getting lots of things done – but they are all things she seems to need, so that isn't misuse. Of course, just because she didn't misuse it doesn't mean no one did. But Source D seems to back up Source B – it suggests people are having surgery for conditions they had just put up with before, but are now getting fixed.*)

Activities

1 Write a sentence about how far Sources C and E agree that the government could not control spending on the NHS.

2 Write a short paragraph explaining how far Sources A, B and D agree about exploitation of the NHS.

74

In the Unit 3 examination, you will be required to answer five questions. You have only one hour and 15 minutes to answer these questions, so the examiners are not expecting you to write huge amounts. The number of marks given in the answer book help you judge how much to write. The time allocation to the right gives a little thinking time before you put pen to paper and a few minutes to read through your answers at the end.

Question 1: 10 minutes	Question 4: 12 minutes
Question 2: 12 minutes	Question 5: 20 minutes
Question 3: 12 minutes	

Here, we are going to look at Question 5. Let's use the sources in the 'Using the NHS' chapter (on pages 72–3) to answer the sort of question you might get in an exam. There are only five sources here instead of the six in the exam, but we can still see how the levels build up.

ResultsPlus
Maximise your marks

Question 5

Examiner's tip: Question 5 is about evaluating a hypothesis. The question will ask you to consider whether the six sources given support a hypothesis. Remember that it does not ask you whether *you* agree with the hypothesis, but whether the sources do. So you are not being asked to write about what you know about the topic. Instead, you need to consider the sources individually and see which side of the argument you would put them on. However, your knowledge is important in assessing the reliability of the sources. If what you know tells you that a source is particularly reliable (or is unreliable) you need say that the degree to which it supports the hypothesis is affected.

'The reason NHS costs were so high was because people misused it.' How far do the sources on pages 72–73 support this statement? Use details from the sources and your own knowledge to explain your answer. (16 marks)

Student answer

The government underestimated how much the NHS would cost. I expect people did take advantage, because things were free and it was new, so they wanted to try it out and see if they really could get free teeth and so on.

Examiner comment

Wrong approach! The question is about whether the sources support the view and the sources have not been mentioned. At best, this would score a couple of marks at the bottom of level 1 for providing some relevant factual information.

Let's start again.

Student answer

Even though Source A is a cartoon, it would not be funny if there was not a real perception that people were misusing the service. Source D talks about a mad rush on cotton wool, which looks like people trying to get what they would buy anyway for free – that's misuse. That is backed up by Source E which tells us that NHS costs were higher than expected.

Examiner comment

The analysis of Sources D and E is very good with clear evidence of how they show misuse. But there is nothing on how any of the five sources show any other possibility for the overspending but misuse. If that had been done, the answer would have moved from a good level 2 (a supported answer), through level 3 (covers both sides of the argument but convincing evidence for only one side) to level 4 (a balanced answer with convincing support for both sides).

![star logo] **Results**Plus
Maximise your marks

So let's do what the examiner wants. The new part is in bold.

Even though Source A is a cartoon, it would not be funny if there was not a real perception that people were misusing the service. Source D talks about a mad rush on cotton wool, which looks like people trying to get what they would buy anyway free – that's misuse. That is backed up by Source E which tells us that NHS costs were higher than expected. **On the other hand, Source D shows us that there was an enormous amount of demand for surgery for previously untreated conditions – and also that people who did not qualify for free treatment before could now get it. The surgery for something you couldn't have afforded to have done isn't misuse. Nor does it sound as if the old lady in Source B doesn't need the things she goes off and gets – she just didn't get them before because she couldn't afford to. Source E backs this up because it shows that costs didn't rise so fast in 1950–1, after the first rush was over.**

This is now a good level 4 answer, with strong evidence from both sides. It is a pity no mention was made of source reliability. Then the mark would have been towards the top of the level.

So let's see if we can address the issue of reliability. The new part is in bold.

Even though Source A is a cartoon, it would not be funny if there was not a real perception that people were misusing the service. Source D talks about a mad rush on cotton wool, which looks like people trying to get what they would buy anyway for free – that's misuse. That is backed up by Source E which tells us that NHS costs were higher than expected. On the other hand, Source D shows us that there was an enormous amount of demand for surgery for previously untreated conditions – and also that people who did not qualify for free treatment before could now get it. The surgery for something you couldn't have afforded to have done isn't misuse. Nor does it sound as if the old lady in Source B doesn't need the things she goes off and gets – she just didn't get them before because she couldn't afford to. Source E backs this up because it shows that costs didn't rise so fast in 1950–1, after the first rush was over.
But it is hard to know how much to trust the sources. The government spending costs are probably right, but they don't give us any indication of why the overspend was – it could just be that they hadn't anticipated how many people were just not getting problems treated. The cartoon is showing the cartoonist's (and the newspaper's) point of view – all we can really say is the paper wanted to support the popular view of exploitation. And while the little old lady in Source B was genuine, who knows how many people can tell stories about their granny tricking the NHS?

This is now a very good level 4 answer.

Note: Remember that Question 5 is one in which your skills of written communication will be judged. To get to the top level you have to write effectively, organise coherently, spell, punctuate and use grammar with considerable accuracy.

Welcome to examzone

Revising for your exams can be a daunting prospect. Use this section of the book to get ideas, tips and practice to help you get the best results you can.

Zone In!

Have you ever become so absorbed in a task that it suddenly feels entirely natural? This is a feeling familiar to many athletes and performers: it's a feeling of being 'in the zone' that helps you focus and achieve your best.

Here are our top tips for getting in the zone with your revision.

- **Understand the exam process** and what revision you need to do. This will give you confidence but also help you to put things into proportion. Use the Planning Zone to create a revision plan.

- **Build your confidence** by using your revision time, not just to revise the information you need to know, but also to practise the skills you need for the examination. Try answering questions in timed conditions so that you're more prepared for writing answers in the exam.

- **Deal with distractions** by making a list of everything that might interfere with your revision and how you can deal with each issue. For example, revise in a room without a television, but plan breaks in your revision so that you can watch your favourite programmes.

- **Share your plan with friends and family** so that they know not to distract you when you want to revise. This will mean you can have more quality time with them when you aren't revising.

- **Keep healthy** by making sure you eat well and exercise, and by getting enough sleep. If your body is not in the right state, your mind won't be either – and staying up late to cram the night before the exam is likely to leave you too tired to do your best.

Planning Zone

The key to success in exams and revision often lies in the right planning, so that you don't leave anything until the last minute. Use these ideas to create your personal revision plan.

First, fill in the dates of your examinations. Check with your teacher when these are if you're not sure. Add in any regular commitments you have. This will help you get a realistic idea of how much time you have to revise.

Know your strengths and weaknesses and assign more time to topics you find difficult – don't be tempted to leave them until the last minute.

Create a revision 'checklist' using the Know Zone lists and use them to check your knowledge and skills.

Now fill in the timetable with sensible revision slots. Chunk your revision into smaller sections to make it more manageable and less daunting. Make sure you give yourself regular breaks and plan in different activities to provide some variety.

Keep to the timetable! Put your plan up somewhere visible so you can refer back to it and check that you are on track.

Know Zone

In this zone, you'll find checklists to help you review what you've learned and which areas you still need to work on.

Test your knowledge

Use these checklists to test your knowledge of the main areas for each topic. If you find gaps or weaknesses in your knowledge, refer back to the relevant pages of the book.

Key Topic 1

You should know about...

❏ Levels and distribution of unemployment in Britain in the 1930s **see pages 10–11**

❏ How the government tried to deal with the problems of unemployment
see pages 12–13

❏ Experiences of the unemployed **see pages 14–15**

❏ The reasons for the Jarrow Crusade, how it was organised and opposition to it
see pages 16–17

❏ The marchers; their effect on public opinion **see pages 18–19**

❏ The effects of the Jarrow Crusade **see pages 20–21**

Key Topic 2

You should know about...

❏ The German invasion of the Netherlands, Belgium and France and the retreat of the BEF
see pages 26–27

❏ The importance of Dunkirk **see pages 28–29**

❏ Churchill and the reasons for British survival **see pages 28–29**

❏ The Battle of Britain **see pages 30–31**

❏ Government preparation for attacks on Britain **see pages 32–33**

❏ The evacuation of the cities **see pages 34–35**

❏ The Blitz and its effects generally **see pages 36–37**

❏ The Blitz on Coventry **see pages 38–39**

❏ How German bombing changed and developed after the Blitz **see pages 40–41**

Key Topic 3

You should know about...

❑ The need for tighter government control in wartime **see page 45**

❑ The use of censorship and propaganda **see pages 46–47**

❑ The impact of the war on the food supply and how the government dealt with it **see pages 48–49**

❑ The war work women did **see pages 50–51**

❑ How women's war work affected post-war employment **see pages 52–53**

❑ What led up to D-Day and how it was planned **see pages 54–55**

❑ The reasons for D-Day's success **see pages 56–57**

❑ The reasons for Germany's defeat **see pages 58–59**

Key Topic 4

You should know about...

❑ Why Labour won the 1945 election **see pages 63–65**

❑ The Beveridge Report and its importance **see pages 66–67**

❑ The attack on the five giants, especially 'want' **see pages 68–69**

❑ Planning the NHS and opposition from the medical profession **see pages 70–71**

❑ The impact of the NHS up to 1951 **see pages 72–73**

Working with sources

Remember, however, that this unit is not just about recalling historical information: you need to be able to interpret and make judgments about historical sources.

As you've studied each topic, you'll have built up a range of skills for working with sources. The table below lists the main areas you should now feel confident in and shows where each is covered in the book. Refer back to those pages during your revision to check and practise your source skills.

	Key Topic 1	Key Topic 2	Key Topic 3	Key Topic 4
Making inferences from sources	Pages 10–11, 16–17, 22	Pages 26–27, 30–31, 32–33	Pages 48–49, 54–55	Pages 63–65
Considering the purpose of a source	Pages 12–13, 18–19, 23	Pages 28–29, 38–39, 40–41	Page 45	Pages 66–67, 68–69
Cross-referencing sources	Pages 12–13	Pages 40–41, 42–43	Pages 50–51, 58–59	Pages 72–73
Evaluating the utility or reliability of sources	Pages 14–15, 18–19	Pages 36–37	Pages 46–47, 60–61	Pages 70–71
Evaluating a hypothesis	Pages 20–21	Pages 34–35	Pages 52–53, 56–57	Pages 74–75

Exam Zone Unit 3B practice exam paper

Here is a practice paper for your Unit 3B exam. The sources that you need to read to answer these questions are provided on pages 80–81. In Unit 3 you need to answer all five questions.

Each question will tell you which source or sources you need to read and refer to. The number of marks available for each question is given on the right. Remember that the Unit 3 exam lasts 1 hour 15 minutes. Plan your time accordingly!

Question 1
Study Source A
What can you learn about the reasons for the Blitz from Source A? (6)

Question 2
Study Source B and use your own knowledge.
What was the purpose of this poster? Use details of the source and your own knowledge to explain the answer. (8)

Question 3
Study Sources A, B and C.
How far do these sources agree about the level of morale in London during the Blitz? Explain your answer. (10)

Question 4
Study Sources D and F.
How reliable are Sources D and F as evidence of how Londoners reacted to the Blitz? Explain your answer. (10)

Question 5
Study all the sources and use your own knowledge.
'The Blitz on London failed.'
How far do the sources in this paper support this statement? Use details from the sources and your own knowledge to explain the answer. (16)

Exam Zone

Background information

The Blitz is the name given to the bombing of British cities by the Luftwaffe from 7 September 1940 to May 1941. It was different from previous bombing raids because it deliberately targeted civilians, not military or industrial targets. The government took many precautions against bombing from the start of the war, including evacuating children. The first, most-often and most-heavily bombed city was London – it was bombed for 75 out of the first 76 nights of bombing (one night it was too foggy to fly). There were bombing raids on many other British cities, for example Coventry and Liverpool. The government worked hard to 'keep up morale' – keep people determined to carry on fighting – despite the bombing.

Source A   From a school textbook published in 1988.

To start with, the *Luftwaffe* [German air force] concentrated on destroying airfields as part of its invasion plan. In September, this policy was switched to one of bombing London. Having failed to beat the RAF [the British air force] *Luftwaffe* planes could only attack at night, when it was harder for the RAF to shoot them down. Bombing cities was intended to break the morale of the British and make them want peace at any price.

Source B   A poster issued by the government in 1940.

LEAVE THIS TO US SONNY — <u>YOU</u> OUGHT TO BE OUT OF LONDON

MINISTRY OF HEALTH EVACUATION SCHEME

Exam Zone

Source C   From the diary of Maggie Joy Blunt, who lived about 20 miles from London, 9 September 1940.

> Raids over London are constant and seem to get worse and worse. Damage and death over the docks and East End have been terrible. But Hitler won't win. We will not be subdued. We will have a better world. Damnation to those who machine-gun our women and children, and they do. Only last week a hundred or more factory girls were killed in this way in their lunch hour.

Source D   From the diary of Christopher Tomalin, a 28-year-old who lived with his parents in London, 15 September 1940.

> Our only shelter from the bombing is the pantry under the stairs: one wall is an outside wall; the other is thin board. I am scared by the indiscriminate night bombing of London and the rest of England. It is obvious the RAF and the anti-aircraft people can't do much about it. We can beat them in daylight, but not when it's dark. How can I, or anyone, sleep under these conditions?

Source E   A postman delivering mail in London, May 1941.

Source F   From a speech by the British prime minister, Winston Churchill, on 14 July 1941, after the Blitz.

> I do not hesitate to say that the enormous change in the opinion of the people of the United States towards making a greater, more effective contribution to British resistance has been largely influenced by the behaviour of Londoners (and the men and women of other cities) in standing up to enemy bombing.

Don't Panic Zone

As the day of the exam gets closer, many students tend to go into panic mode, either working long hours without really giving their brain a chance to absorb information, or giving up and staring blankly at the wall.

Look over your revision notes and go through the checklists in Know zone to remind yourself of the main areas you need to know about. Don't try to cram in too much new information at the last minute and don't stay up late revising – you'll do better if you get a good night's sleep.

Exam Zone

What to expect in the exam paper

You will have 1 hour and 15 minutes in the examination. There will be five questions and you should answer all of these. There will be between six and eight sources in a separate source booklet; some of these will be written and some will be illustrations.

Question 1 is an inference question worth 6 marks. It will ask what a source is suggesting, usually phrased as 'What can you learn from Source X?' You should spend about 10 minutes on this question. For an example see page 22.

Question 2 is a source analysis question worth 8 marks. It will ask you about the purpose of the source, for example 'Why was the source produced?' or 'Why was this photograph used?' You should spend about 12 minutes on this question. For an example, see page 23.

Question 3 is worth 10 marks and involves comparing or cross-referencing up to three sources. The question will usually be in the form 'Do these sources support the view that…?', 'How far do these sources agree about…?' or 'Do Sources A and B support Source C about…?' You should spend about 12 minutes on this question. For an example see pages 42–43.

Question 4 is worth 10 marks and asks you to evaluate the utility or reliability of two sources. For example, 'How useful or how reliable are Sources D and E?' You should spend about 12 minutes on this question. For an example see pages 60–61.

Question 5 is a judgment question worth 16 marks. It will start with a statement and then ask 'How far do the sources in this paper support this statement? Use details from the sources and your own knowledge.' You should spend about 20 minutes on this question. For an example see pages 74–75.

Meet the exam paper

This diagram shows the front cover of the exam paper. These instructions, information and advice will always appear on the front of the paper. It is worth reading it carefully now. Check you understand it and ask your teacher about anything you are not sure of.

Print your surname here, and your other names afterwards. This is an additional safeguard to ensure that the exam board awards the marks to the right candidate.

Here you fill in the school's exam number.

The Unit 3 exam lasts 1 hour 15 minutes. Plan your time accordingly.

Make sure that you answer all questions.

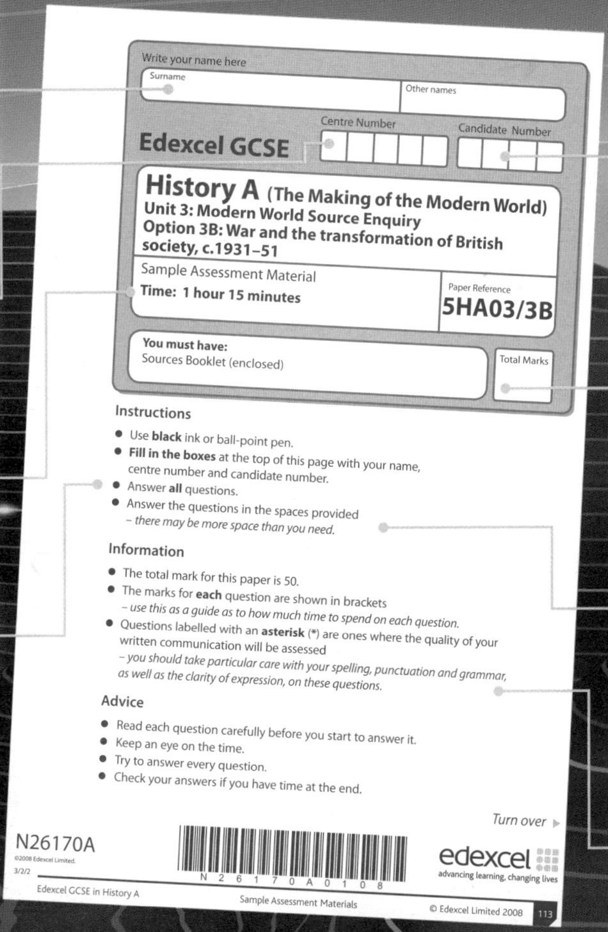

Here you fill in your personal exam number. Take care to write it accurately.

In this box, the examiner will write the total marks you have achieved in the exam paper.

Don't feel that you have to fill the answer space provided. Everybody's handwriting varies, so a long answer from you may take up as much space a short answer from someone else.

Remember that in Question 5 the quality of your written communication will be assessed. Take time to check your spelling, punctuation and grammar and to make sure that you have expressed yourself clearly.

Write your name here

Surname

Other names

Centre Number

Candidate Number

Edexcel GCSE

History A (The Making of the Modern World)
Unit 3: Modern World Source Enquiry
Option 3B: War and the transformation of British society, c.1931–51

Sample Assessment Material
Time: 1 hour 15 minutes

Paper Reference
5HA03/3B

You must have:
Sources Booklet (enclosed)

Total Marks

Instructions

- Use **black** ink or ball-point pen.
- **Fill in the boxes** at the top of this page with your name, centre number and candidate number.
- Answer **all** questions.
- Answer the questions in the spaces provided
  – there may be more space than you need.

Information

- The total mark for this paper is 50.
- The marks for **each** question are shown in brackets
  – use this as a guide as to how much time to spend on each question.
- Questions labelled with an **asterisk** (*) are ones where the quality of your written communication will be assessed
  – you should take particular care with your spelling, punctuation and grammar, as well as the clarity of expression, on these questions.

Advice

- Read each question carefully before you start to answer it.
- Keep an eye on the time.
- Try to answer every question.
- Check your answers if you have time at the end.

N26170A
©2008 Edexcel Limited.
3/2/2

Edexcel GCSE in History A

Sample Assessment Materials

© Edexcel Limited 2008   113

Turn over ▶

edexcel
advancing learning, changing lives

Answer all questions.

This question paper is about the impact of the Blitz.

Look carefully at the background information and Sources A to F in the Sources Booklet and then answer Questions 1 to 5 which follow.

1 Study Source A.

What can you learn from Source A about the German bombing raid on Coventry, November 1940?

(6)

The live question paper will contain one further page of lines.

(Total for Question 1 = 6 marks)

In Unit 3 you need to answer all five questions on the paper.

Each question will tell you which source or sources you need to read in the sources booklet.

The number of marks available for each question is given on the right.

The sources booklet will provide you with some background information that will help you to put the sources in context.

Read the detail about the origin and date of each source carefully before studying the source.

Background information

In the years 1940-41 Britain suffered numerous German bomber raids which mainly targeted towns and cities. Hitler believed that the Blitz would destroy the morale of the British people and force Britain out of the war. Some historians believe that the German raids did seriously reduce the morale of the British people. Other historians claim that there were far worse effects.

So, what was the worst effect of the Blitz on the British people?

Source A: From a broadcast on Berlin radio, 16 November 1940, about the air raid on Coventry.

More than 500 planes took part in the greatest attack in the history of aerial warfare. About 500 tonnes of high explosive bombs and 30,000 incendiary bombs were dropped. In a short time all large and small factories were set on fire. The German airforce struck a violent blow in return for the British raid on Munich on the night of 8 November.

Source B: From a British newspaper, the Daily Herald, 16 November 1940.

Coventry

The bombing of Coventry was as foul a deed as Hitler ever ordered. His airmen were instructed: 'Don't worry if you cannot reach your industrial targets. Bomb and burn the city. Never mind if you hit factories. Hit houses. Have no scruples about military objectives. Kill men, kill women, kill children. Destroy! Destroy! Destroy!'

Heil Hitler! Heil bloodshed! Heil pain!

Zone Out

This section provides answers to the most common questions students have about what happens after they complete their exams. For much more information, visit www.examzone.co.uk

When will my results be published?

Results for GCSE summer examinations are issued in the third week in August. January exam results are issued in March.

Can I get my results online?

Visit www.resultsplusdirect.co.uk, where you will find detailed student results information including the 'Edexcel Gradeometer' which demonstrates how close you were to the nearest grade boundary.

I haven't done as well as I expected. What can I do now?

First of all, talk to your teacher. After all the teaching that you have had, tests and internal examinations, he/she is the person who best knows what grade you are capable of achieving. Take your results slip to your subject teacher, and go through the information on it in detail. If you both think that there is something wrong with the result, the school or college can apply to see your completed examination paper and then, if necessary, ask for a re-mark immediately.

Bear in mind that the original mark can be confirmed or lowered, as well as raised, as a result of a re-mark. After a re-mark, the only way to improve your grade is to take the examination again. Your school or college Examinations Officer can tell you when you can do that.

I achieved a higher mark for the same unit last time. Can I use that result?

Yes. The higher score is usually the one that goes towards your overall grade. You do not need to ask Edexcel to take into account a previous result. This will be done automatically so you can be assured that all your best unit results have gone into calculating your overall grade.

How many times can I resit a unit?

You may resit a unit once prior to claiming certification for the qualification. The best available result for each contributing unit will count towards the final grade. If you wish to resit after you have completed all the assessment requirements of the course, you will have to retake at least 40 percent of the assessment requirements (that means two units). Please note that if you take a resit as one of the two units in your final assessment, the score you get will be counted – even if your original score was higher.

Glossary

Term	Definition
air raid shelter	Somewhere built, usually underground, where people can go to be safer from bombing.
Allies	Allies are people or countries who work together. In the Second World War, the 'Allies' was the name given to the countries that fought together against Germany and its allies.
artillery	Large guns or cannon, that fire over long distances.
bail out	Said by pilots about jumping out of a plane, usually with a parachute, while the plane is still in the air.
barrage balloons	Large balloons, fixed in place with ropes or cables, that were flown above important places to stop the enemy flying low enough to bomb them accurately.
benefits	In this sense, used to mean payments made to people from a National Insurance scheme they have paid money into while working.
blackout	Not showing lights anywhere at night – covering doors and windows, turning out street lights, etc.
Blitz	The name given to the bombing of British cities by the German air force from 7 September 1940 to May 1941.
cabinet (the)	The prime minister of Britain and government ministers, meeting regularly to make decisions.
censorship	Stopping people from passing on certain information – in newspapers, radio broadcasts, private letters and even conversations.
conscription	Making people join the armed forces or do war work.
Depression (the)	The period from after the Wall Street Crash in the USA when world economies were all in trouble and there was a lot of hardship and unemployment.
eligible	Qualified to get or apply for something.
employment exchange	A place where unemployed people went to register as available for work and to see if there are any jobs.
evacuate	To evacuate a place is to clear people out of it.
evacuee	Someone who is evacuated – sent away from a dangerous place.
export	To export something is to sell it to another country.
hunger march	The name given to various marches in the 1930s by unemployed people hoping to be given work or other help.

import	To import something is to buy it from another country.
manifesto	A list of the political beliefs of a person or group of people.
means test	The inspection that people had to go through to show they were poor enough to qualify for 'the dole' – state assistance for the very poor.
minister	The person in the government in charge of a ministry, for example the Ministry of Education.
ministry	The place where people run all the government work to do with one particular area of life, for example education.
propaganda	Giving people information in order to make them think or behave in a particular way.
public baths	Places with washing facilities (sinks and baths) for people with none of their own to use.
public meeting	A meeting in a public place that anyone can go into.
radar	Short for **RA**dio **D**etection **A**nd **R**anging, a way of detecting objects a long way away in the dark or fog by bouncing radio waves off them and picking up a picture of their shape.
rationing	Restricting how much of something people can have.
refugee	A person who has been driven out of their home/country, usually by war or persecution.
relief	In this sense, it means help given to people who are homeless or desperately poor.
sandbag	A bag made from cheap sack-type fabric, about the size of a pillowcase, filled with earth or sand. Sandbags are stacked up against buildings to lessen the damage done in flooding or by an explosion.
trade union	An organisation of workers set up to help protect their rights.
Treaty of Versailles	The treaty between Germany and the Allies at the end of the First World War that limited Germany's armed services and took away much of the land Germany took in that war.
voluntary group	A group of people who work at something or provide some kind of service for free.
workhouse	A place where homeless people can live, but were families were split up, the work was hard and people were fed very little food of the cheapest sort.

Acknowledgements

Published by Pearson Education Limited, a company incorporated in England and Wales, having its registered office at Edinburgh Gate, Harlow, Essex, CM20 2JE. Registered company number: 872828

Edexcel is a registered trademark of Edexcel Limited

Text © Pearson Education Limited

First published 2009

12 11 10 09
10 9 8 7 6 5 4 3 2 1

British Library Cataloguing in Publication Data
A catalogue record for this book is available from the British Library.
ISBN 978 1 846905 51 3

Typeset by eMC Design Ltd
Original illustrations © Pearson Education Ltd 2009
Illustrated by Peter Bull Studio
Printed in Great Britain at Scotprint, Haddington

Acknowledgements

The author and publisher would like to thank the following for permission to reproduce photographs:

(Key: b-bottom; c-centre; l-left; r-right; t-top)

akg-images Ltd: 26, 37; **The Art Archive:** Bodleian Library Oxford 64; Eileen Tweedy 47l, 49; **Bridgeman Art Library Ltd:** E. H. Henington 13; Colin Moss 6, 19; Royal Naval Museum, Portsmouth, Hampshire, UK 47r; Bert Thomas 45; **Corbis:** Bettmann 9, 24, 34, 38; Hulton-Deutsch Collection 7, 8, 11, 17, 18, 20, 46, 51, 62, 68, 81; David Pollack 25; Underwood & Underwood 63; **Getty Images:** Central Press 39; Fox Photos / Harry Todd 44, 50; Picture Post / Kurt Hutton 15; Popperfoto 41; Popperfoto / Rolls Press 57; Topical Press Agency / Edward G. Malindine 52; Topical Press Agency / Warburton 53; **Imperial War Museum:** 33; Cundall, Charles Ernest RA 28; **© News Group Newspapers Ltd:** Peter Brookes, The Times, 1 Nov 2000, British Cartoon Archive, University of Kent, www.cartoons.ac.uk 21; **Solo Syndication:** Associated Newspapers Ltd / David Low, Evening Standard, 19 Aug 1940, British Cartoon Archive, University of Kent, www.cartoons.ac.uk 31, / David Low, Evening Standard, 19 Jun 1944, British Cartoon Archive, University of Kent, www.cartoons.ac.uk 40, / David Low, Evening Standard, 19 Jan 1945, British Cartoon Archive, University of Kent, www.cartoons.ac.uk 59, / David Low, Evening Standard, 7 Jun 1945, British Cartoon Archive, University of Kent, www.cartoons.ac.uk 65, / Illingworth, Leslie Gilbert, Daily Mail, 17 Feb 1943, The National Library of Wales 67, / David Low, Evening Standard, 15 Jan 1948, British Cartoon Archive, University of Kent, www.cartoons.ac.uk 71, / Ronald Niebour, Daily Mail, 24 Aug 1948, British Cartoon Archive, University of Kent, www.cartoons.ac.uk 72; **TopFoto:** HIP / The Lordprice Collection 80

Cover images: *Front:* **Alamy Images:** Trinity Mirror / Mirrorpix

The author and publisher would like to thank the following for permission to reproduce copyright material:

Tables
Table on page 10 adapted from *British Unemployment 1919-1939*, Cambridge University Press (Garside, W. R.) Table 2, p.5, © Cambridge University Press 1990, reproduced with permission; Table on page 15 from *The Twentieth Century*, Macmillan Education (Hamer, J. 1988) pp. 106-7, reprinted by permission of the author; Table on page 16 from *Modern World History*, Heinemann (Hewitt, T. and Shuter, J. 2001) p. 270, reprinted by permission of the publisher and Tony Hewitt; Table on page 52 from *Social Trends in Britain since 1900*, 2nd Edition, Macmillan (Halsey, A. H. ed. 1988) p. 169, A. H. Halsey, *British Social Trends since 1900*, published 1972, Macmillan, reproduced with permission of Palgrave Macmillan; Table on page 73 adapted from *The Health Service in Great Britain*, Oxford University Press (Ross, James Stirling 1952) p. 315, by permission of Oxford University Press.

Text
Extract on page 12 from Unemployment. HC Deb 04 November 1932 vol 269 cc2127-210, http://hansard.millbanksystems.com/commons/1932/nov/04/ unemployment, Parliamentary material is reproduced with permission of the Controller of HMSO on behalf of Parliament; Quote on page 21 from Unemployment (Jarrow). HC Deb 05 November 1986 vol 103 cc1058-66, http:// hansard.millbanksystems.com/commons/1986/nov/05/unemployment-jarrow, Parliamentary material is reproduced with the permission of the Controller of HMSO on behalf of Parliament; Quote on page 26 adapted from a story written by Agnis van Loon, reprinted by permission of Trevor Griffin; Quote on page 30 adapted from an article about Frank Walker-Smith, *Derby Evening Telegraph*, 2001 (Slater, B.), Derby Telegraph; Quote on page 32 from Pat Ashford from Mass-Observation diary, August and September 1939; Quote on page 33 from Eileen Potter from Mass-Observation diary, 25 June 1940; Quote on page 33 from Edward Ward from Mass-Observation diary, 8 August 1940; Quote on page 35 from Eileen Potter from Mass-Observation diary, September 1939; Quote on page 35 from Tilly Rice from Mass-Observation diary, 5 December 1939 and 6 February 1940; Quote on page 37 from Christopher Tomalin from Mass-Observation diary, 15 September 1940; Quote on page 37 from Pam Ashford Mass-Observation diary, 15 September 1940; Quote on page 40 from Maggie Joy Blunt from Mass-Observation diary, 25 June 1944; Quote on page 41 from Edward Stebbing from Mass-Observation diary, June 1944; Extract page 81 from Maggie Joy Blunt from Mass-Observation diary, 9 September 1940; Extract page 81 adapted from Christopher Tomalin from Mass-Observation diary, 15 September 1940; Sources from the Mass Observation Archive reproduced with permission of Curtis Brown Group Ltd., London on behalf of the Trustees of the Mass Observation Archive. Copyright © Trustees of the Mass Observation Archive; Extract on page 35 adapted from Evacuees in World War Two – the True Story by David Prest, reprinted by permission of the author; Quote on page 38 adapted from the account of Ted Simmonds, with kind permission from Rev. Pam Crane; Extract on page 46 adapted from Churchill's top secret call girl, *Daily Mail*, 10 October 2008 (Hennessy, V.), Daily Mail; Extract on page 47 from *Make Do and Mend*, prepared for the Board of Trade by the Ministry of Information, Crown Copyright material is reproduced with the permission of the Controller of HMSO and the Queen's Printer for Scotland; Extract on page 48 from *The Times*, 26 April 1941, © The Times/NI Syndication Ltd. 1941; Extract on page 66 from the official notes of a Cabinet meeting on 15 February 1943, http://www.nationalarchives.gov.uk/releases/2006/january/january1/default. htm; Extract on page 67 from Social Insurance and Allied Services. HC Deb 18 February 1943 vol 386 cc1964-2054, http://hansard.millbanksystems.com/ commons/1943/feb/18/social-insurance-and-allied-services, Parliamentary material is reproduced with the permission of the Controller of HMSO on behalf of Parliament; Extract on page 72 from Origins of the NHS, http://www. nationalarchives.gov.uk/cabinetpapers/alevelstudies/origins-nhs.htm; Interview on page 73 from Dr John Marks at http://www.nhs.uk/Livewell/NHS60/Pages/ JohnHenryMarks.aspx, Reproduced by kind permission of the Department of Health, © Crown Copyright 2009.

Every effort has been made to contact copyright holders of material reproduced in this book. Any omissions will be rectified in subsequent printings if notice is given to the publishers.

Disclaimer

This material has been published on behalf of Edexcel and offers high-quality support for the delivery of Edexcel qualifications.
This does not mean that the material is essential to achieve any Edexcel qualification, nor does it mean that it is the only suitable material available to support any Edexcel qualification. Edexcel material will not be used verbatim in setting any Edexcel examination or assessment. Any resource lists produced by Edexcel shall include this and other appropriate resources.

Copies of official specifications for all Edexcel qualifications may be found on the Edexcel website: www.edexcel.com